SIX REAL WAYS TO MAKE MONEY ONLINE

TABLE OF CONTENTS

COPYRIGHT PROTECTIONS	
INTRODUCTION	5
CHAPTER ONE: HOW TO MAKE MONEY BLOGGING	9
Different Types of Blogs Are Given Below	12
Use Blogging for Profit	17
The Advantage of Blogging	26
How to Make Money Blogging – Successfully	30
CHAPTER TWO: HOW TO BLOG FOR PROFIT	37
What Is Blog Creation	37
Hiring a Blog Creation Service	41
Why Should I Create a Blog	43
How to Blog for Profit	46
Publicize Your Blog	52
How to Make People Click Ads on Your Blog	60
Make $100 a Day from Your Blog	65
CHAPTER THREE: HOW TO MAKE MONEY IN STOCKS	71
What is Stock Exchange	77
Stock Market Technical Analysis	79
How to Make Money in Stocks	81
Stock Options	84
Invest In Stocks - The Better Way	87
Strategy for Investing in Stocks	91
Why Invest in Stocks	97
Best Time to Invest in Stocks	100

Why Investment is a Must for Every Individual	103
CHAPTER FOUR: HOW TO MAKE MONEY IN STOCKS COMPLETE INVESTING SYSTEM	106
How to Make Money on Stocks Whether They Go Up or Down	110
Pros and Cons of Stock Trading	113
The Pros and Cons of Preferred Stock	116
CHAPTER FIVE: HOW TO DEVELOP THE TIME AND MONEY MANAGEMENT	120
Top three Money Management: How to Ruin Your Financial Life	152
Money Management as Techniques to Protect Your Money	157
7 Key Points to Money Management Success	160
Time Management	165
Time Management - An Essential Tool	168
What Does Time Management Have To Do With It	171
Time Management Software Solutions	175
Time Management Goals	178
Time Management Examples	181
The Ideology of Time Management	184
CHAPTER SIX: HOW TO CREATE A WEBSITE	188
Benefits of creating a website	191
Website Hosting	194
Best Ways to Make Money with Your Website	197
CONCLUSION	200

COPYRIGHT © 2017
COPYRIGHT PROTECTION

All rights reserved. No part of this publication may be reproduced, distributed, or transmitted in any form or by any means, including photocopying, recording, or other electronic or mechanical methods, without the prior written permission of the publisher, except in the case of brief quotations embodied in critical reviews and certain other noncommercial uses permitted by copyright law.

INTRODUCTION

You can start making some cash online even if you are not yet prepared. Go through this eBook properly, for information in this eBook will help you generate an online source of income. Making money online from your home has never been easier. This has been made possible because the Internet world is growing tremendously in the "online money-making" field, that's why many people have had their lives changed completely for the best. Anyone willing to put in those hardworking hours will definitely succeed in the Internet marketing world. Yes, it won't be easy trying to generate a good source of income online, but it is definitely possible with some extra hours and hard work.

While there are plenty of ways and means by which you can make a bit of money online with ease and for free, it's important to be realistic about how much you'll make and the effort you'll need to put in. Money doesn't grow on trees anywhere on Earth and the web is no exception, so while you may make a success of yourself online given time, you can't expect to earn a fortune overnight or get rich by doing nothing at all.

In order to reach goals and fulfill desires, our mind and our body manage to apply principles and techniques that influence our daily activities and decisions. Since our early childhood, we have been accumulating information through the process of observation. We have acquired knowledge by gathering information. We have filtered our intelligent assessments by testing our knowledge.

We have also adapted our behavior, harmoniously with our psychology, in a modus operandi that complies with our choices, our decisions, our agreements and our rejections. Along the way, we have accumulated a few principles that are deeply associated with our observations in the learning curve of our existence and we are constantly using them to modify our lines of action.

As long as we evolve with needs, the success in a business will rely on our choices. Our choice to make money online will require using our behavior. In the choice theory, the behavior is said to be central to our existence. Some people will give the best of their effort to succeed in a business for the love of money. The money will provide food so they'll never deal with starvation. While nice clothing and jewelry attract admiration, a nice house defies the need for a simple shelter. Vacation and travel will help them breathe another air. Savings and retirement plan forge personal safety and peace of mind for themselves and their loved ones.

Love is a reason for accessing another level of success because it increases your connectivity and the sentiment of pertaining to another level of society. The next step is power in connection with significance and competence. Then comes the sensation of freedom and your autonomy and independence. Later on, life becomes fun. We have gradually taken you to the Maslow Triangle.

You can make money online using your behavior as seen from another angle. We will just mention a few notions among the many. As some people will repeat that knowledge is the power we will invite you to use perseverance. This attitude defines your persistence to reach your goals and to overcome obstacles. Then comes discipline. We are talking about self-discipline, which is the capacity to motivate oneself notwithstanding a negative passionate state. Along comes the go-getter in you as a person who acts and gets things done. Meanwhile, you need to balance your emotions with patience. Some people say that patience is a virtue because it will help you overcome pain, avoid complaints, and manage the loss of temper, irritation, or the like. The previous character evolves in harmony with this one: be an open-minded person, meaning someone who is willing to consider ideas, opinions, and arguments purely on their merit.

A human being is bound by principles that lead the daily routines. Those principles evolve under the more familiar notions of aptitude and attitude. Behaviorism defines the inner spirit that will control the evolution of the mind and the action-reaction we take in response to stimuli at various level of interaction with life. Making money online could be a matter of survival but without good behavior, we may miss the key factors that will lead to our success.

CHAPTER ONE
HOW TO MAKE MONEY BLOGGING

The concept of blogging has permeated every nook of the internet's virtual world. A blog is synonymous to the modern day diary that claiming not to know about it officially makes one naïve and outdated. Save yourself from being labeled ignorant and start filling yourself with information regarding this basic question - 'What is a blog?'

A blog is a contraction of the word weblog, which is actually a kind of website maintained by a specific person by regularly uploading it with informational entries. Depending on the weblog goal, the information may be opinion based or may be validly supported by existing facts in the internet, with references provided. Technological advancement has allowed blog postings to include a video or a desired graphic in the site. The writer is nowadays referred to as a blogger and the word blog is presently being conveniently used as a verb. To be able to sufficiently answer the question 'what is a blog?' you need to learn how the blogging process works and the technicalities involved.

A term frequently mentioned whenever people talk about blogs is the niche. Those who intend to make their blogs cater to a specific group of consumers serve a definite niche. Staying with the intended niche more or less guarantee readership. It will be easy to navigate a blog that consistently talks about dogs, or about fashion, or about real estate than the one with a mixture of topics. For those who are not into marketing and just would like to have an internet journal, personal blog diaries can narrate about anything under the sun, without the need to retain visitors. This main difference about the major types of blogs is an essential knowledge to sufficiently respond to the query 'what is a blog?' You can definitely earn from your blog through advertising, and advertisers choose according to their market niche.

Blogging has continuously been evolving in such a way that it inevitably interlinks with the different aspects of society. The issue on personal freedom of expression was posed after an airline company fired one of its flight attendant allegedly for keeping a blog about her flight duties. It is also common to hear about news stations correcting its previous news because of a massive blogging reaction. Blogs certainly have contributed to enabling the people claim their rights on correct information. So whenever you get the question 'what is a blog?' you should be prepared for a meaningful discussion.

A blog does not necessarily have to be always for public consumption. There are corporate blogs created for business purposes to be used by a group of employees under a specific company. Such types of blogs are maintained for internal communication and business culture enhancement goals. There are also instances when corporate blogs are externally used for public relations and marketing.

The purpose for blogging may not always be to reap profits. However, taking into consideration the economic conditions and the vast potential of turning a harmless hobby into a money-making machine, who wouldn't want to explore blogging for money? Then, whenever someone throws the question 'what is a blog?' at your direction, you can confidently respond with the right information.

DIFFERENT TYPES OF BLOGS ARE GIVEN BELOW

There are different sorts of blogs although most blogs are a little bit of all types. So the type of blog you build is limited only by your imagination. You may also want to do a bit of research to see what type of blog styles are currently out there. For example, some blogs focus on one topic that may be very general like animals where other blogs will be more specific such as a blog about only dogs or even a blog about only German shepherd dogs.

When you are organizing your content for a blog the smaller your focus the easier your organizing will be since the topic will be very narrow it will be easy to choose categories.

When you are focusing on a larger, more general topic, choosing categories may become more difficult.

When building a blog there are typically 9 major areas that all blogs fall into business, culture, community, politics, religion, science, travel, online diaries, and gossip. Again, when looking at these categories you will see how many blogs will cross into multiple areas at different times depending on the topic of the most recent post. Even business blogs can have gossip or politics or even religion depending on the voice of the person creating the blog and also depending on the business the blog is for.

When you are considering setting up your blog another thing to consider is the program or software you will use to create it. Most blogging software tends to have links to other blogs created with the same software easily available to other users. Wordpress blogs tend to have links to other Wordpress blogs and blogger blogs tend to have links to other blogger blogs built right into them. This is the same for social networking types of blogging platforms. Sites like

Livejournal and MySpace allow users to surf from blog to blog based on friend links and similar content.

Blogs can be more than just articles that you type up and post to the internet. There is also a photo or video blogs. In these blogs, the information is usually conveyed using pictures or videos. With a video blog, the blogger might record themselves talking about the topic that day or maybe record an event that is occurring that they want to share with the world. They then take that video and post it to their blog and make it available for everyone to watch.

While most blogs are created by a company or an individual there are blogs that allow many people to participate in providing information. Some that are gaining in popularity are geographic blogs. These blogs focus on information pertaining to a specific region of the world, may it be a country, a state, a city or one neighborhood. Then everything on the blog would be directly related to that specific area.

So you see, blogs can be as unique as the people that create them. It is best to determine the purpose of your blog before you get started and consider what you hope to accomplish by having one and therefore what the best platform will be for your particular type of blog. But you also want to remember not to get too caught up in the planning. A blog in your head does you no good at all. Part of the point of blogging in the first place is to get your information out onto the internet where the world can see it. With a little bit of planning and preparation, you will be able to get started on your blog very easily.

The personal blogs are mostly used to update the bloggers' family members, friends, and relatives about the latest events going on in their lives. Some people also use personal blogs to vent their frustration by expressing their feelings and thoughts.

Rules of Conduct

- You will be responsible for all the activities done on your blog. This includes the comments your viewers leave and the comments left by you.
- Make it clear to all your visitors that no abuse will be tolerated.

- You should immediately clear off all offensive and annoying comments.
- If you find a person giving negative or offensive comments then caution them immediately.
- If you want to say some personal things to someone, don't use blogs to do so.

Now, have you got the answer to what is blogging? Those who know how to make full use of blogging find it really interesting. Moreover, blogs can be financially beneficial for your business and organization. On the other hand, you will receive negative comments if you show your anger or frustration on your blog. Keeping your blog clean and avoiding negative comments will help you build a good reputation. It will also create a positive impression on those people who read your blog.

USE BLOGGING FOR PROFIT

Making your blog work for you;

Starting a blog for personal expression means that it doesn't really matter how many views you get, if you are searching at running a business based on marketing blog then views are of the utmost importance. So how do you get those views?

The basics of blogging;

A blog is an internet publication which usually takes the form of a diary or journal, although they can also be used for news and reviews about specific topics or products. Blogs usually include personal comments, viewpoints, and experiences as well as often containing links, videos, and images. Lots of people begin keeping a blog as a way of expressing personal or professional views.

Blogs, however, can quite easily be used as a platform for writing about and marketing your business or products online. At the moment blogs are experiencing a huge level of popularity across all sectors of the internet and can be an effective and very inexpensive way to reach a wider audience.

One of the best things about blogs is that people often read them at leisure. Clients and consumers are becoming more and more wary of advertising but will happily read a blog as long as it has some interest to them on a personal level. Most of the world's top companies use blogs to deliver more value and a more personal touch when trying to introduce people to their companies a strategy that seems to be producing good results.

Where to start?

Starting a blog is surprisingly simple all you really need is the time to write and somewhere to post your blog. To start with you will obviously need a topic or theme for your blog. A great way to get some good ideas for your topic is to look around the internet first and see what other people are talking about on their blogs. Generally speaking, you want to have one core theme for your blog similar to the way that many newspapers have columnists that talk about one specific topic. This topic can be very narrow or very wide but it is important to ensure that your readers know what kind of things you are likely to cover otherwise they are likely to read one article they are interested in and then stop following your blog if you begin talking on a topic that has no interest to them.

Once you have a general outline of what you want your blog to be about you need to start thinking of what you want to name your blog. Short catchy names are great but make sure to try and include some clues as to what the blog covers in the title. This will make it much easier for people to find your blog.

Of course deciding on a topic and working out a cool name will be of no use if you don't have a place to post your blog. There are a huge amount of places around the internet where you can post a blog nowadays, some of which are free and some of which charge a fee for use. If you can't find a place to put your blog I would suggest simply doing a quick Google search for blog hosting sites and then doing a little research into which option is best for you. Of course, if you have your own website already then you can also post your blog right to its own page there. One big advantage of this is that it can also bring people in to have a look around the rest of your web page if they like what they see on the blog.

Things to remember about writing;

Writing a blog is by no means rocket science, but there are a few things that you should try to keep in mind to make sure your blog is easy and enjoyable for your followers to read.

1. Make sure your English (or whatever language your blog is in) is up to a certain standard. While society cares far less about perfect grammar, spelling, and syntax than it did in the past it is still important to at least ensure that you make your blog legible. Obviously, most websites and blog sites have a built-in spell check too so there really is no excuse for bad spelling.

2. Try to express yourself clearly. Blogs are not really formal writing and are definitely not supposed to be an essay. Try to keep your sentences and paragraphs reasonably short and keep your language light and easy to read.

3. Think about adding videos and/or pictures to your blog. Research has shown quite clearly that people engage much more readily with pictures and especially with videos than with walls of solid text.

4. Even if you are promoting a product, company or service try to minimize the amount of advertising you have in each blog post. It's OK to give people an option to buy your product or through an affiliate link buy a product you are talking about and which may interest them, but having a huge amount of "spam" links and banners all over your page is a huge turn-off. After all, as we have already said people usually come to blogs looking for information or a little light leisure reading, not to be bombarded by your sales pitch.

5. Be engaging. Try to be a normal person. Even if you are selling a product or marketing a company people relate better to real people with real stories and ideas than they do to someone who sounds robotic and one-sided.

How to promote your blog;

All your hard working finding the perfect blog idea and name as well as a great place to post it will come to nothing if you can't get people to read it and finding readers is all about promoting your blog. Just writing good content and posting to a good blog hosting site is not really enough to get you a good audience. There are literally millions of blogs out there with people posting new blogs even as you read this so unless you have a good way of promoting your blog you will have trouble getting readers.

There are a few choices open to you when considering how to promote your blog. You can advertise your blog by placing links to it or mentioning it in emails and on social media and forum pages. Other possible options include getting blog hosting or article hosting sites to review your blog and hopefully post it on their front pages or higher on their search rankings as well as things such as entering blogging competitions. Finding people who blog about similar topics can also help you as you can partner up with them and do some form of cross-promotion where you send people to their blog and they return the favor.

The key to keywords;

For people who know roughly what they are looking for but not where to find it search engines such as Google and Yahoo are extremely helpful. For the very same reason, these search engines are great for the blogger too. Many search engines use algorithms which search for keywords in a website or blog. Even if your content is good if you don't use the right keywords then people still might not be able to find you. Correct keywords are essential and should reflect what you want people to be thinking about when they find your blog. A good way of making sure you have the right kind of keywords is to do a search for the keywords you want to use and see what results you get. If the results are close to what you are offering you've hit the nail on the head if not try rethinking your choice of keywords.

Keeping it neat;

Keeping your business blog clean and uncluttered is important for drawing in customers. Think about it if you go into a store or even onto someone's website the first thing you notice is what the general layout looks like and as they say first impressions count. If you went into a store and there was random aisles full of odds and ends lying around would you be as interested as if the aisles were neat and you could find exactly what you were after easily?

For this reason, it is often good to use a slightly more spartan approach with a business blog than you would with a personal blog. If you are lacking ideas about functional yet simple backgrounds and color schemes for your blog searching around the internet to find some sites that have got a good look can be helpful.

Don't push your message too hard;

The whole idea of a company or marketing blog is to promote your company and/or your chosen products. That being said consumers can easily be overwhelmed or put off by constantly being blasted by adverts or sales messages. If you overload your blog with links, advertising material (including banners) and sales pitches then you are likely to simply frighten away the customers you have worked so hard to get visiting in the first place.

Providing readers with "Value" is a great way of gaining and keeping their trust and making sure they keep coming back. The easiest way to provide this value is by producing good blog material that is as unbiased as possible, whilst obviously being kind to your own product, and that is valid and up to date. There is nothing wrong with promoting the fact that you have a new product or line, but try to keep it from sounding like you are simply there to sell your readers something without giving them anything worth reading into the bargain.

Value you can add;

Most companies offer giveaways, free samples and special offer codes in their marketing material. There is no reason you can't also give away these things on your blog, and in fact, if you do it gives people a great incentive to keep tuning in so they don't miss one of your great offers. Other values that should be added to a good blog include things such as good advice on how to achieve what the customer wants to achieve. For example paint companies posting tips about how to get that perfect finish or health food Company's blogging about great news ways to use their products in recipes. All of this added value turns you from a seller into a trusted expert and source of news and information.

THE ADVANTAGE OF BLOGGING

These days to have a successful site you need a blog. A blog has content and Google loves content. If you have a well-written blog you will get more visitors to your site. These days' people are turned off by pages just trying to sell with no other really valuable information. People look at the blog to see if the site knows the subject and will buy more easily.

There are just also numerous advantages of running a blog for business; yet, the greatest advantage is that of bringing in and building significant visitors of visitors to your site on the daily basis. And of course, this would mean generating better product sales for your organization.

Promotes and Sells Your Product

Indeed, blogging nowadays has become a significant part of doing business.

And no organization owner in his sane mind ought to miss out on the immense potential of doing corporation through running a blog. One way would be to just start blogging by creating and using your individual blogs and ultimately be ready to advertise and sell your goods and companies to thousands of website visitors every day. And inside the event that you just already have a well-liked weblog web site, you'll surely get countless of guests each day.

Becomes an Entirely free Marketing Tool

So, who says blogging does not offer any benefit for the corporation when it presents itself like a free tool for advertising one's corporation, item or service? Without a doubt, technology has gone a long way and with the modern trend of using blogs, a great deal more and more companies have started to create their very own blog sites, to possess the ability to share inside the open, the quality of their items and services. The threads in the forums could also talk about the quality of your product or service or the quality of your job they provide.

Successfully Responds To Customer Needs

Business owners or organizations could also use running a blog to serve as catalogs that will be linked inside the Web and would then be connected to plenty of websites inside the World Vast Web. With this, the typically asked concerns of new clients will be successfully answered through these blogs which could also be a perfect way to introduce new merchandise or new features of an outdated product or service.

Gets to be a Marketing Tool

These days more and more sites are realizing they need a blog, these days' blogs are used for just being a social site to a full-blown blog selling thousands of items... Plainly, blogging and enterprise match properly with each other. Nonetheless, emphasis will really need to be put on building a top quality Blog. A blog might probably perhaps be published with so lots grandiose in phrases and yet still seem empty. These kinds of blogs can never be useful to an organization.

Another advantage of blogging for the enterprise is always that it is so truly quick and easy to create. Not to point out that it is exceptionally affordable. That is why it is so difficult to understand why some websites until now which have not realized the importance of making their own Blogs. Even if you're technologically naïve, you will have the capacity to put in place your private weblog.

All you ought to do is possess a software application set up on your Internet site, adjust the settings and voila! You've acquired your private Blog to use for promoting your website and making it bigger, needless to say!

Enables Client Accessibility to Facts

No matter what kind of blogs your organization may perhaps potentially properly maintain, there's one apparent benefit of running a blog for business, and that is it enables for buyers to assess the site and blog and buy from you.

What is even superior about it's that it could possibly even usher in immediate revenue for that site. Build a blog and they will come to look at it. Then they will have a better understanding of the subject, and you will have a better chance to sell to them.

HOW TO MAKE MONEY BLOGGING - SUCCESSFULLY

Your most important assets are dedication and patience. Approximately 9% of bloggers are able to make a part-time income from blogging, and an even smaller percentage of 4% are able to make over $10,000 a month from blogging (six figures a year). However, don't get discouraged. With consistent effort and passion, you can easily make at least part-time income from blogging. Here are the most effective tips on how to make money blogging:

Create a blog with the appeal

The first step is to have a blog. It is preferable to have your own website and it is easy to purchase one. Try to add something to your blog that makes it unique, intriguing or appealing. Spend a good portion of time making sure that your design and layout is appealing to others and will not be distracting or hard to look at.

Produce valuable content

What you are writing needs to be useful and valuable to others. Whether it is entertaining, evokes emotion, gives them factual information, or produces them with opinions, your content needs to have a purpose and something must be taken from it by the reader.

Find your voice

You need something that will separate you from other bloggers and find your own unique way of speaking is going to attract more readers. Your writing voice is the tone and diction you use that will make you memorable and keep people interested in what you have to say. If you sound generic, people will lose interest quickly and you will not reach as many people as you wish to. Voice normally comes naturally to writers, but try to focus on bringing out aspects of yourself into your writing.

Connect with your audience

The audience is extremely important and connecting with them will do wonders for your blog. Learn as much as you can about what you are trying to communicate to your audience and put yourself in their shoes. Think about what you would want to hear if you are searching out your own content and go from there.

Interact with other bloggers

Connections are important in the real world and in the blogging world as well. Establishing relationships with other bloggers will give your blog more attention and support. Comment on other blogs with positive remarks, especially blogs that focus on the same topic as yours. This will lead to you feeling more successful and interactive with the blogging community.

Design an Attractive User-Friendly Blog

Nothing can be more frustrating than a site that is hard to navigate hence the importance of designing a blog that is easy not just for you but also for every other visitor you receive. It is helpful to focus on website design when starting your blog just to make sure that what you have at will be attractive to your visitors and easy to work around. It is the foundation of the blog thus the importance of choosing elements bound to work to your advantage.

Add some personal touch to the blog

This is also important in setting you apart from the rest of the bloggers. Customize the blog so that it is as unique as it possibly can. Blogging platforms such as WordPress give you the benefit of customizing your own blog so it stands out. You will have a beautiful blog without having to spend money on web developers. Consider using headers and logos on the site to improve the look and encourage time spent on the blog.

Endeavor to learn to write

The one mistake bloggers make is to write anything that comes to mind. However, the quality of your posts and the content you create will highly determine the kind of traffic your blog attracts. Giving attention to your grammar and sentence structures and having a clear picture of what exactly you are about to say should guide you in proper writing. Introductions and anecdotes should be included and different writing techniques must be evaluated to ensure your content will attract and maintain the attention of your readers.

Boost traffic by installing plug-ins

They are important not just in attracting traffic, but also encouraging their stay and turning old visitors to come time and again. The plug-ins are simple to add on some of the blogging sites and you should have enough and those you feel will do justice to your blog.

Take advantage of Google analytics

It is a useful tool in tracking the website progress. The best thing about this kind of tracking is that you will always know where you need to make changes and what you need to give more attention to depending on the reaction your visitors have towards your posts. Simple changes can go a long way in improving your blog and the results it fetches you hence tracking progress is of importance.

Be consistent

Consistency is extremely important. Readers will want to hear from you regularly and will lose interest fast if they see that you have not posted in a week. Try to post at least once every two days. A successful blog needs a lot of time put into it and you need to be engaging with your readers as much as possible.

Having money coming from more than one place will actually help you make more. You have to remember that once you have gotten people interested in your blog, your blog is a platform and there are options available to you for making money. Some of them include:

Advertising: You can make money through advertising by the use of display ads, which appear on your blog. These ads should be related to your blog's content so that people will get even more engaged. Google AdSense is also something to explore!

Giveaways and reviews: A giveaway or review is when a company supplies a blogger with a product and then that blogger gives it away to a reader or reviews it in a blog post.

Sponsored posts: A sponsored post is when you talk about a product in detail and a company will pay you for it. It is important to keep these to a minimum so that you don't lose readers. Readers will know when you are being paid to talk about something which is often a turn-off. However, once in a while they are a good stream of income.

By putting in an hour or more every day, you will find that you are gaining more followers and people who are interested in your blog. Eventually, you will see that your streams of income are growing and you are making more money with each passing day. The important thing is not to lose hope and to keep trying. Being passionate about what you are doing will make it easier to keep at it every day and eventually you will see positive results!

CHAPTER TWO
HOW TO BLOG FOR PROFIT

WHAT IS BLOG CREATION

What can you make with your blog creation? There are many people like students, parents, kids, internet marketers, a business owner who all want to create something. Some call it a website where I sell things, others call it my online portal to share my knowledge and others call it to review sites that only if visitors click through my link, do I get paid. These are all known as blogs or websites and to me it's a blog creation. A webpage where it's about what you want with updates along the way.

If you were to create a blog but didn't know what to build, here are some ideas:

- Review Sites
- Blog Recipes
- Share videos about your life
- Give feedback on your local places
- Start a group on Facebook and have them leave comments on your blog.
- Start a non-profit blog where you seek donations to help a worthy cause.
- Build a sharing blog where you help people out with ideas and what to blog about
- Design and develop blog themes and sell them on your blog.
- Blog about your top 10 things or what you want to do before you pass away from this earth. I could go on but I hope that you are generating some ideas for yourself and how you want to see this blog creation come out. It

is really up to you, you have to vision yourself out there and making plans and then taking action on them. And all the while regardless of the craziness happening all around you, you're blogging your passions and services and whatever else you can offer for free and paid.

Some people will have a blog where they come up with videos they love and curate that content. It's called video curating or video content curation. It's what big sites do all the time and you can easily get into doing the same thing online for your blog or website. These things work well if you are really into typing and expressing yourself. Just be sure that you are helping to your audience more than the video so they can get your insight and help from you directly. That is your special touch so to speak and everyone has their own unique twist.

Another form of a blog creation is a podcast blog where the webmaster/podcaster promotes his or her message about what they want. And then they will upload to their blog and some blog feed plugins will submit your content to Apple. Then users on the Apple devices will search for content related to you and download, thus another visitor to know about your website and an opportunity to promote on your podcast your blog URL.

Some blog creation websites you can use are:

- Blogspot.com
- Facebook.com
- Blog.com
- Posterous.com
- Tumblr.com
- Weebly.com
- Wikispaces.com
- Wetpaint.com
- LiveJournal.com

There are other online blog platforms beyond just this list. There are also paid blogging platforms where you have to pay to join. Some of these networks are a lot better when it comes to avoiding spam blog communities.

Remember when it comes to blog creation, it's about your expression onto a reality that others can see to a certain degree.

HIRING A BLOG CREATION SERVICE

Creating a blog is not as easy as it looks. Sure it is fairly simple to use a free blogging platform such as Blogger or WordPress and use their templates, but if you want something more than that, you could likely benefit from hiring a blog creation service.

A blog creation service can customize a blog to give it a professional look and feel and seamlessly integrate it into your existing website. That way your blog is part and parcel of your site, while still giving you access to the many great features of a blogging platform such as WordPress.

WordPress is the world's leading blogging platform. It is free, search engine friendly, and allows you to moderate comments, turn comments off, add images, polls, access other great plug-ins, and much more. WordPress is the easiest platform to use and does not require any knowledge of code to add content. It is also simple to add and delete users and set permissions.

The term blog comes from the word weblog. They can be like an online journal where the writer can express opinions, make announcements, and readers can make comments providing feedback.

Blogs really took off in the past decade or so. Personal blogs have waned a bit in popularity in recent years in the U.S. with the advent of social media sites such as Facebook and Twitter. However, for businesses, they are still very important.

Having a blog can make a big difference in terms of traffic for a website. Blog posts can generate traffic through search engines, typically through what is known as long-tail search, and through people linking to them. One single blog post, if properly targeted and executed, can generate thousands of visitors to a website. This is very valuable as this amount of traffic can lead to a lot of new customers to the business.

Your blog can also become a source of authority on your product or service, helping to promote your reputation. You can also have links to your Facebook, Twitter, and other social media site accounts on your blog posts allowing your blog to have an even bigger impact and reach more customers.

Blogs can be a great way to promote new products and services. You can also provide company news or write interesting or useful articles to attract readers. With WordPress, it is easy to self-manage and adds content if you do not want to pay a blog writer.

WHY SHOULD I CREATE A BLOG?

It's my opinion that basically, everybody should create their own blog. It's not as hard as people think. Technology and human ingenuity have served to make the internet so much more intuitive and easy for the layperson to access. Here are some reasons I believe everyone should have a personal (maybe business) blog.

- Blogs are part of the new business model. It is common knowledge that traditional media models are dying. Newspapers all across the country are going down because they haven't adapted to this new paradigm. Though I don't believe they will ever disappear completely, I think it will be a decline from here on out, and then level off at some point.

- A blog really is (not 'like') IS your Avatar to the online world! It is your interface and a form of self-expression that has the potential to reach millions. A myspace or Facebook page does not have the potential to go viral like a blog page can. Not even close. And it's fun!
- A positive and negative, the internet has the characteristics of a truly new frontier where humans can gather information. There is still plenty of room to operate out here, and though competition is fierce in many obvious places, there are still areas (niches) out there which are still relatively pristine, untouched and waiting for you to find them.
- Connections: Business, friendship, relationships, informational, there are myriads of reasons why people create blogs. The reasons for creating one are as varied as the personalities of humans! But who could not benefit from more connections, whether it be friends or for business?

- Ad revenue. Yes, you can monetize your blog. Again, there is a myriad of ways to do this. This itself is easily a full-sized book of information itself and is a topic I plan to delve into further into the future. Stay tuned!
- According to Google itself (which should know these things), barely 30% of the world population is online. Judging by the most recent information, there does not appear to a world trend of declining internet usage. Even the United States, which is easily the most internet-saturated country in the world, still has room to grow. I hope you can easily see how the internet is here to stay.

If you haven't seen by now, I believe everybody should have a blog online. The internet is not going anywhere, it is only going to grow, and a blog is in a perfect place to grow with it. Blogs are the new online sensation these days for many good reasons, some of which I explain above. One thing I didn't mention: It is common knowledge among the web developer community that Google Loves Blogs, which means blogs tend to have a higher search ranking for keywords than traditional websites, in general. So if you want your website to actually be found by Google, you are not making a bad person or business decision to go with blog creation!

HOW TO BLOG FOR PROFIT

Blogging can be a fun activity and it can also be profitable. However, blogging for profit requires quite a different strategy compared to blogging for fun. If you are blogging for profit or plan to do so, then here are 3 simple but essential steps you need to do to succeed in making money from your blog.

Set Up Your Own Blog Site

If you are blogging for profit, you must have your own blog site, and not rely on a free blog from free blogging sites like blogger.com, blogspot.com, MySpace.com, etc. The reasons you need your own site are:

(a) It projects a more professional and serious image of your blogging,

(b) You can add a lot more useful and essential plugins to give functionality and efficiency to your site, and

(c) You have full control and ownership over your work.

My personal preference for a blogging platform is WordPress as it is easy to set up, easily modifiable and has almost limitless themes and plugins to make your blog more aesthetic, functional and almost 100% automated. Some plugins are essential tools to make your blog site more visible and profitable.

Choose a specific niche to blog, preferably one that you are passionate about. Only then will you have the energy, enthusiasm, and knowledge to blog regularly.

Blogging for profit also means that you'll need to discretely add advertisements like Google AdSense or ClickBank to your site, and to promote some great and related products through your blog postings from time to time.

Blog Regularly

Blogging is fun and is often addictive. Once you get the hang of it, you'll want to do it as often as possible.

The key to a profitable blog is consistency in your posting. Set a daily schedule of 1 to 2 hours to post in your blog. Post sensibly and make sure that your postings contain information that is useful for your readers.

Do not post simply for the sake of posting. It is not necessary to have a long post. Sometimes, several one or two paragraph postings can be more beneficial and welcomed than a single long post.

Keeping people interested in your blog whether it's for your business or personal blog is important to attract many visitors many blogs have died because people simply have lost interest. The main reason for this lack of interest, naturally, is the lack of content that should publish the blogger. By adding good material regularly and frequently push to your blog to be positioned on search engines, and that is essential for the survival of any blog.

You may be wondering, what does that mean? How many blog entries I do in a week? How do I make these entries, are consistently good? In this newsletter, we will see step by step all that.

Publish in your blog often?

Post in your blog often means you must write enough content to keep readers interested. Obviously, people do not like returning to a blog that has not been updated in months. They want to see interesting publications, and then they go to check the blog next week to see if there is more content, knowing that it will not be a waste of time.

How many publications I do on my blog?

This is an imperative question to answer and that really depends on the purpose of your blog. If it is a personal blog, once or twice a week is fine. For a blog about politics, sports, music or religion, should ideally be between 3 and 4 publications per week. Commercial blogs should have at least 2 publications, although it would be best to have 4 per week.

Is very important to remember that the key is good content, find information relevant to the reader and publish it. Post often, try to find the balance between the quantity of publications and quality of content. Why create 4 poor quality each week, when you can publish only 2, but excellent quality each week?

How do I create articles for publication that are of quality and have a consistent basis?

Simply to follow a pattern of writing that is solid, maybe you're not a writer then it becomes a little more difficult. So I will give you a little help.

1. Choose a topic that is interesting both to you and your readers.

2. Think carefully what you write on the subject. That makes it easier to publish quality articles in your blog. Arrange all the items you are considering for publication, even before you start writing it!

3. Before writing the content selects some keywords that have little to do with your blog, if you use the keywords naturally throughout its publication that will increase your blog's position in search engines.

4. Start writing your article not limited to a certain amount of words. Just do naturally and if during the writing process you

feel frustrated or difficult, just take a break and relax. You may do so later, more calmly; the important thing does not get discouraged.

Why Is It So Important Publication Frequent?

Blogs have created to be part of the market for individuals and businesses. They are used to get an opinion about an issue and engage readers. And these readers need to have something that makes them want to return frequently to a blog... that, in general, is due to the quality and frequent publications.

Winning and keeping visitors is not the only reason to post often on your blog, making search engines locate it in a good position is another good reason to publish regularly, is more likely with each publication on your blog offers some words or phrases with keywords that are popular in your niche, logic says that the natural keywords that you can put on your blog are the best.

Similarly, the more keywords you have in your publications is more likely to be detected by search engines and as that site is located, is more likely that you have a high ranking in a search engine.

The frequency of publications in the blogs can be very easy; provided that the person is doing (the blogger) will take the time enough to make a plan for what to write. So take a moment to think about your article and then just write it and publish it.

PUBLICIZE YOUR BLOG

Profitable blogging depends on 2 important factors. The first is the quality of your blog; the second is how extensive you can reach out to the people out there.

So, once your blog site is up and running, do not feel shy to promote it to your friends and colleagues. Publicizing and marketing your blog site is an essential part of blogging profitably. Include your blog site URL in your name cards and hand them out liberally to friends, colleagues, and acquaintances, even to strangers and people you are meeting for the first time.

If you are passionate enough in your subject matter, they will see and understand your eagerness in sharing your passion with them.

You also need to expose your blog site to as many people as possible online. You can do that through various methods, such as advertising, using social networks, and collect a following for your blog via newsletters sign-ups and RSS. There are many WordPress plugins that help to link your postings from your site to other social networking sites like Facebook and Twitters.

Publicizing a blog is not as hard as publicizing a website, yet, it is still quite an arduous task. Marketing your blog can be done as you write the article; all you have to be is a little clever about it.

Get Search Engine Friendly

Your first task to complete on your marketing strategy is to make your blog search engine friendly. By this term, the experts are referring to how easily the search engine picks up your blog. To your blog, search engine friendly is essential to create a blog that is ranked and recognized by search engines.

How? This is pretty easy to do. All you need do is to create relevant and appropriate post titles, which include your article's subject. Page archiving is also useful as it will come up automatically with relevant post page names, leaving you free to concentrate on the fun bit - the article's content.

Moreover, use relevant terms in the main body of the article and be specific, so don't go off tangent. It's vital not only to optimization that you keep to the point, but to gain the reader's interest too. Add links and anchor text too in order to optimize your blog.

Social Networking

Whether you love it or hate it, you cannot doubt that it is a useful internet tool. Many bloggers are keeping their fans updated via Twitter and Facebook. You can either update these manually by phone or computer or add a link to your twitter account on your blog. Add an **RSS** feed to Twitter and anyone who is linked to your twitter account will receive a feed stating that you have new website news.

To network join other similar groups or blogs in order to publicize your blog among your particular audience. Networking is absolutely vital to getting known on the World Wide Web.

Submit Your Blog

Submitting your blog address to search sites and directories will help get your blog recognized in the wider blogging community. Every time you blog, you can also submit your address to Ping websites, which inform the search engines that you have new website news available. This is still needed to be done for many blogs, all except WordPress.

Feeds and Emails

Keep your readers updated by subscribing to site feeds, enabling them to be informed of the arrival of new articles. Installing goodies such as email this eBook will enable readers to subscribe to have it in email form and pass it on to their friends and family.

Always Comment

Get your readers involved by enabling a comment box. Always try to write back to them and also leave comments on other relevant blogs. It is vital to make sure you are a fully active participator of the blogging world if you want to get anywhere.

Product Reviews

If you have a personal blog, then you could do product reviews of things that you actually use.

This could be things like; hair products, electronics, movies, video games, etc. However, you wouldn't want to keep it to a theme. So if it is going to be about hair products, then keep it in that general area of beauty products, or something along those lines.

This way you will be able to cater to your audience better. That does not mean you cannot have multiple sites for all of your interests, the more the better actually.

Postings Ads

A lot of people will create a "hobby" blog that talks about a specific topic. However, they normally don't do a lot of product reviews, so to make money from that blog the best thing they can do is have a section of the site that is for ads that cater to the visitors of the site.

This means if the site is about model cars; then they can have ads to other websites that pertain to model cars. You would price these ads depending on the amount of traffic you are getting.

You would start off with for every 1000 people a month you get to the site, each ad block would be worth around the $10/month mark.

Make sure you do not have too many ad blocks though; 1 across the top, and maybe 6 - 8 along the right side.

Just let people know who do advertise that it is for a set period of time, let's say 3 - 6 months, and then once that time period is up, you can check how much more traffic you are getting, and charge them accordingly.

Six Real ways to Make Money Online

I have seen too many blogs filled to the brim with ads, ads like Google AdSense, text link Ads, banners, links, and much more. When I see a blog that has five or six banners in a row at the bottom of the sidebar or blog, lined up unevenly, just makes me want to run away screaming. And what's to worry about is that even in these ads is something to readers that they will be interested in what is the theme of the blog.

It is one thing; some people simply have no interest in blogging do so at all. All they want to do is earn money in cash (which causes an overflow of ads). Well, it does not work that way. You need determination and you have to be in it for something more than money. Admittedly, I too blogged for money - but I also do it because I like it, and I've had many blogs before this that had not monetized at all. In fact, I just start with my blogs again a couple of months ago.

If you are going to make money blogging, you have to learn to make some money for you, a) you have to write content and get people interested in them, and b) you have to organize your ideas into an organized, professional. Of course, there's more but those are the main ideas.

If you have five or six ads lined up unevenly, you're not going to make money. Instead, you are going to scare away your visitors. Nobody wants to see that. Think about what programs are making more money for you, and those who do not. Then eliminate all that do not bring any benefit, and place the ads that make money, spread in various parts of your site and not bother your readers.

People hate ads and more so if it clogs the blog making it difficult to read your blog - in order to avoid this, limit the number of ads and banners to two or three, and definitely no more than five. Try putting them in different spaces and see what ads work best - but believe me, making a few cents is better than losing all your visitors.

HOW TO MAKE PEOPLE CLICK ADS ON YOUR BLOG

Regardless of the possibility that you have huge activity on your site, it doesn't imply that you will get huge amounts of snaps to your advertisements (Google AdSense or some other). You may trust me or not but rather there are a couple of ways you may expand snaps to your advertisements without breaking any promotion program rules... A few people simply put promotions anyplace on their site and are sitting tight for an enormous income. Be that as it may, it doesn't work along these lines. You have to comprehend what's going on with you or you should take in it from your own particular mix-ups and lose a ton of time.

I. Optimize you ads.

Some time back Google has posted on their blog a decent article about ideal promotions arrangement. In any case, you should realize that there is no such thing as the best place for any advertisement on any blog! Treat your guests the way that you need to be dealt with. In the event that you are excessively hostile they will close web program before reading any substance and obviously, you will get no snaps to your promotions! You need to try different things with various promotion organizations and areas to perceive what works best with your site traffic.

There are a couple of guidelines you ought to follow:

- Ensure that your ads fit subject you expound on.
- Pick strong shading for the title of the ad to make it seen by your readers.
- Keep in mind that excessively showy ads are overlooked by most clients - influence them to fit your site.
- Put your ads in places that most readers will quit perusing for some time (after some awesome thought, conclusion). Spots they need think or test what you have written.
- Choose one of the procedures portrayed below to make your substance work for you.

II. Make your content work for you!

There are a couple of techniques to take after when you are composing content for your blog. Some may sound minimal amusing and some are harder to utilize yet it truly works! You may pick other methodology for each of your next three posts and test what makes your guests clicking generally ads.

Technique Number 1 - the hardest one

Make your substance so educational and fascinating that it would change the life of your guests (or finally offer an answer for an issue they need to determine). In the event that they adore your article such a great amount of, a large portion of them will need to state much obliged. Some of them will compose doltish remarks "much appreciated", "incredible article", "I cherish you..." and so on that convey nothing fascinating to subject of your post and won't let you procure a buck... Be that as it may, some more astute ones realize what the ads are for and would click them for saying: "much obliged - extraordinary substance, you should make a living of composing such a great posts!"...

Technique Number 2 - not as hard

Check what intriguing individuals are discussing on long-range informal communication sites. Compose short fascinating articles about it. Be that as it may, don't put too much data in it! Compose just some concise most intriguing realities and influence individuals to state "Hello... what a fascinating subject... however, I need to know more..." Ensure that your ads fit subjects you expound on. Individuals will snap to discover more data. In this technique, you can't put any connects to extra assets or individuals will click it rather than your ads.

Technique Number 3 - probably the easiest one...

Make extremely intriguing titles for your articles. Be that as it may, make content as exhausting as could reasonably be expected. Influence them to long and difficult to peruse. Try not to arrange it, don't utilize records, sections. Influence individuals to shout "Let me out of here!!!" They will need to leave your site as quickly as time permits. Sadly some of them will close web program with your website and will need to promptly disregard your article, however... some of the truly exhausted guests will click anything they see to leave your site and flee, the admission the better. In the event that you will have some fortunes, they would click your ads and you will get your income...

The third one may seem like a joke yet I have used to visit a couple of blogs throughout my life that is utilizing it! It truly influenced me to tap the ad to discover anything that might be all the more fascinating that went to blog! Tell me what is working best for you and good fortunes with utilizing it on your blog!

Being paid to post

This can be done 1 of 2 different ways:

1. You can have your own site, and people pay you to post on your blog about their site, or product.

2. Another way is; you get paid to post blog posts, and comments on their blog, etc. Basically giving them content to their site

Now that you have read this chapter, you understand 3 different blogging for profit ways that you can make money at; Product review website, posting paid ads on your blog and being paid to create blog posts on your site or someone else's site.

If you do all these six steps right, and you blog regularly and consistently, I can assure you that you'll be making money from your blog within 6 months or at most a year.

MAKE $100 A DAY FROM YOUR BLOG

Making $100 a day from your blog is really easy. In fact, you should feel very dumb if you're not.

A successful person makes reasonable goals and achieves them.

If need to be successful in anything you have to make short-term and long-term goals. The same thing goes for making money from your blog. You have to force yourself to create the goals and do everything you can to achieve them. Sometimes, that might mean staying up an extra few hours at night or even missing sleep entirely.

A list of reasonable daily blog goals (you can decide how many days a week)

Six Real ways to Make Money Online

By the end of today, I will have......

- Written at least two blog posts
- Responded to all comments left on my blog
- Visited the websites of the people who left comments on my blog and will have posted a comment on theirs.
- Visited other blogs in my niche, will have left appropriate comments and will have built a relationship.
- Started an email relationship with at least one other blogger.
- Met my monetary goal for the day
- Found a way to add at least 10 subscribers to my newsletter list.
- Found some way to get at least 1 - 2 backlinks to my site.

Reasonable daily monetary goals

In the beginning, it is reasonable to set a low monetary goal. But as time goes by, $100 a day is not hard at all. I am going to list the different stages of monetization.

Stage 1: Between 1 - $5 a day

Most of your money is going to be made through pay-per-click (PPC) advertising. This would include programs such as AdSense and Auction-Ads.

Stage 2: Between 5 - $20 a day

At this point, you should be consistently making a few dollars a day from advertising programs on your blog. If you are following the above daily steps, you should have a consistent readership of your blog. This means that your Alexa ranking and your Search Engine rankings are getting you to a point where you can start to get paid to write reviews of products or websites.

There are a few ways to get money by doing reviews. The easiest way is to post in forums a lot and use a signature.

Your signature can say something like "I will review your site on my blog, PM for details.

When you first start doing reviews, you might have to do a few for free. Then you can start charging $5 - $10 per review. If your customer is satisfied, they will probably pay you to review their other websites. (In the beginning, it might be worthwhile to exchange reviews).

Stage 3: Between 20 - $50 per day

By this time, your Alexa ranking should be 100,000 or lower and your Google PR should be at 5. If this is true about your site, you can start charging people for putting links on your site. A link on a PR5 site should run about $5/month. A review on a high traffic blog can cost anywhere from $10 - $20 your blog is also at a stage where you can start selling banner ads.

In this stage, you are to have a pretty good following. This is a following that is now starting to trust you. This is a good time to start promoting affiliate programs. As long as the affiliate programs you are promoting are in your niche, you should be making a lot of money. Don't forget to advertise your affiliates in your newsletter.

Stage 4: Between 50 - $100 per day

You have probably been following the above steps for at least 7 months to a year. Your Google PR is at 6, your Alexa ranking is lower than 50,000 and you are ranking pretty high on some keywords in the search engines.

In stage 4 you are making decent money. You have become a professional blogger and a trusted member of your community. You are ready to create an ebook on how you make $50 - $100 a day. At this point, people are ready to pay you for consultations and will definitely pay you more money for reviews and advertising space.

It is time to write information products on "tips and secrets" in your niche.

Stage 5: $100 and over a day

You are now almost a Guru in your field. You have finished your information products and have submitted them to affiliate sites like Clickbank. You now have people selling your products for you and visiting your blog on a daily basis.

Because of your success, medium size websites and podcasters want to interview you. You are on your way to being able to quit your day job.

Your Short-Term Goals

Your short-term goals are the 5 stages I listed above. Once you have reached a particular stage, you need to write in the exact date you expect to reach the next stage.

CHAPTER THREE
HOW TO MAKE MONEY IN STOCKS

Investing is stocks are one of the largest ways that people look to make residual income when it comes to investments. In fact, many people use stocks as a way to build on their retirement funds and trusts. It is imperative to know how to invest in stocks even if you are using an investment company or a brokerage to handle your trades.

Knowing how to invest in stocks can keep you informed and help you to make wise investment choices. When looking into how to invest in stocks the first thing to do is look into the various things that are going to affect the market. There are some things that will affect the market on a widespread basis and there are some that are going to affect only a particular portion of the market. Knowing this information is going to assist you in determining where to invest and how to invest your money on stocks of interest.

Once you have some of the stocks that you are interested in it may be a good idea to get the trends and patterns that are formed by the movement of that particular stock. This will tell you when to purchase the stock, when to sell the stock and how to predict when certain stocks may become more viable investment options.

These patterns and trends require some mathematical computation. As a result, these are best done by entering data into an application designed specifically for marketing analysis. These applications are readily available and many stock investment software applications provide reporting functions that can help with these stock analysis.

Knowing how to invest in stocks is the best way to protect yourself your investment as well as yourself. In order to minimize the financial risk at the same time you increase your potential gain, it is best to be an active participant in your portfolio. Know what the market is that you are investing in, which stocks and what types of factors have a direct effect on that particular market as well as the market, in general, this will help to reduce the level of which you will lose your investment.

You do not need to be an expert in stock investing in order to be actively involved but you will probably need to invest some time in researching terms, trends, and how to spot things that will potentially bring about a greater return for you and your investment.

Whether you are investing as a way to earn extra money, as a job, or to save for retirement being able to actively participate or trade on your own is something to consider seriously. This helps minimize the risk whether you are investing on your own or you are investing through a brokerage firm. Stocks especially cheaper stocks can contain a greater amount of risk due to fluctuations that larger more stable companies. While this does present a less stable trading environment you can see a greater amount of potential and use a reporting of the patterns and trends of the stocks is part of knowing how to invest wisely on the market.

You must have seen the phrase 'stock options' in classifieds. Several companies offer stock options, in addition to other compensations, to their employees. What are stock options? How are they beneficial to people? How are they related to stock market trading? We will first study the employee stock options and then understand the stock options in stock market trading.

Stock options offer you the right to purchase a specific number of your company's shares at a specific price. Stock options offer threefold benefit to the company. First, the employees who hold the stocks of the company become stakeholders in the company and therefore have more responsibility. Stock options are useful in retaining good employees. People who hold stocks also feel that they are getting a better compensation.

The strike price is the discounted price of the company shares at the time of offering the facility to employees. As the employee would not exercise his options at the same time, the profits in terms of greater assets as the prices go up. The negative, that is, the price reduction is possible only when the company performs poorly.

Stock options come with a vesting period. This is the amount of time that is offered to the employee to actually purchase the shares. Either he can purchase all shares at a time or he can purchase them in parts, spread over the vesting period. Vesting period gives you the opportunity to delay the purchase of shares. As you would be purchasing shares at a discounted price, you can purchase them at different intervals so that you get them at a lesser price than the market. You can either hold the shares or sell them at the market price through the stock market.

Stock options come with an expiration date. You have to exercise your stock options before the date or you lose your rights over the stock. Stock options are priced at the internal value of shares, thereby allowing you to purchase shares at rates that are much lower than the share market value. If you are leaving the company, you can utilize only the vested options. You lose your rights over the share options that have not been vested already.

Stock options are a subset of call options. A call option is an agreement wherein the seller has the obligation to sell off some financial instruments, such as stocks, to the buyer as and when the buyer is willing. On the other hand, the buyer is not obligated to purchase the stocks based on the will of the seller. Call options in stock market trading allow a person to buy the rights of, instead of the actual, shares and sell it at whatever price the market offers. Call options are valid only for a certain period. These are useful if you are sure that the share price is bound to go up. Also, if you are holding stock in call options, you will not be getting the dividends on the stock unless you actually purchase it. The bright side is that you own them at a much lower price than the market price.

WHAT IS STOCK EXCHANGE

What is stock exchange? People who often hear the words stock market or investments in the news know that stock exchange (SE) is the second half of the famous four-letters that bring millionaires and millions to mind: NYSE. With the recent prominence of Wall Street in political circles, people are beginning to realize it's not just millionaires crediting Nasdaq and NYSE. If there's any place where millionaires and paupers are made in the blink of an eye, it's not a Vegas casino (although we all know that's as good a place as any); it's the stock exchange.

Understanding what is a stock exchange and how it works lies in understanding the role stock brokers play in the various markets. Unlike your regular department stores, the assortment of goods - stock, bonds, and currencies - traded in the various markets for financial instruments have prices that are constantly fluctuating. News updates, political statements, expert opinions - these, among many other things - cause movements in the prices quoted on a stock exchange. And much like any other person doing business in any market, an investor wants to make profits. Understanding what is stock exchange means you know you make money when you selling your investments at a price higher than what you paid for it.

Although stock brokers are simply the middlemen that carry out the actual buying and selling on behalf of investors, they're in a unique position to provide sound investment advice to these people. They deal directly with the goods in question and their exposure to the situations in the particular stock exchange they work in makes them excellent financial advisors. However, if you head a stock broker's advice, you should know that it can go either way - you can become a millionaire or a pauper. Unless it's an automated one like the Forex Tracer, stockbrokers are humans and are prone to errors in judgment.

STOCK MARKET TECHNICAL ANALYSIS

In order to earn good returns from the stock market, investors need to find reliable, accurate and effective systems to make accurate predictions and remain ahead of market movements. A lot of modern trading systems rely on both fundamental analysis and stock market technical analysis. To be successful in stock trading, current trading systems are used to attain the best results. The stock market technical analysis is a method used by experts to predict stock trends. The stock market technical analysis is particularly helpful for long-term investors who need accurate and reliable platforms that can guarantee the best results.

Despite the fact that the market is volatile, investors and experts with access to the right market information can lower their risks by effectively bracing themselves for future stock movements. This can be achieved by looking at past performance and taking into an account earning potentials.

What is stock market technical analysis? This is a technique used to forecast future trends of stock prices by examining the previous data particularly the prices and volume of shares traded. It's worth mentioning that the market technical analysis only takes into account the price and volume behavior of stocks. This is because volume and price are the two most important factors that give an indication of how particular stocks will behave in future. Experts who use this market technical analysis believe that the latest price of a stock already carries plenty of information that can be used in determining future investment decisions.

According to this market technical analysis, external happenings such as news or a high rate of unemployment don't significantly affect the prices of stocks. It's important to point out that technical analysis relies heavily on patterns and charts with an assumption that investors tend to have put forward specific actions and responses.

Despite the fact that a lot of experts and investors find this market technical analysis a reliable approach, fundamental analysis is also helpful as well. In the case of fundamental analysis, predictions for future stock prices and stock movements are based on all real and current data. Some of the important considerations that fundamental analysts use to calculate the value of stocks include the overall state of the economy, industry factors such as financial reports and management performance. Other factors include national economic indicators that have a huge impact on what happens in the stock industry.

HOW TO MAKE MONEY IN STOCKS

If you've been considering buying stocks and wondering how to make money in stocks then you will probably already know the most basic principle of investing. Buy low and sell high! This is how the money is made from trading stocks when you are investing. And then there is Warren Buffet's #1 rule which is "never lose money".

Buying Yourself a Piece of the Pie

When you decide to purchase a share or shares of stock in a particular company, you are actually buying yourself a piece of that company. You have then entitled yourself to pro-rated profits earned while holding the asset. Generally, there are two ways which are money is made on the stock market.

Unless you are into day trading or short-term trading, you will most likely be holding onto your stocks for long-term gains.

Therefore, let's say a company with an affordable $10 stock price grows at a rate of 20% for a ten year period, which is possible. The stock that was purchased for just $10 per share would be worth a little more than $600 per share after a decade assuming the same price-to-earnings ratio is maintained by Wall Street. Depending on how many shares purchased, that could make a nice payday for the investor.

Earning Money with Stock Dividends

In addition to the money the investor would make over the long-term as described above, they would also receive dividends. Dividends are payments made by a company to its shareholders. When the investor receives their dividends check, the funds are then yours to do whatever they want. It may be re-investing back into the company by purchasing more shares or taking a nice vacation with the family.

Researching Possible Stock Picks

Now that the basics of how money is made using the stock market have been covered, we will delve into some things you should know before purchasing any stocks that seem enticing. First of all, you want to shop for companies that are undervalued. Next, look for stocks that have price-earnings ratios lower than those of their peers.

Of course, watch the news, especially financial reports and specials on the stock market. There is a lot of good information to be had by paying close attention to the media. Wall Street has been known to overreact to bad news and drive a stock price down lower than it really should be. This presents a good buying opportunity for a stock investor. Next, check out the head honcho, find out who is running the business and where the top executives worked in the past.

Once you have done your initial research, there is still more to do if you want to ensure a good stock pick for your portfolio. An investor may want to look at the balance sheets of the companies interested in. Things that make a company a good prospect are positive cash flow, low debt and consistent above average earnings. Finally, know when to drop a loser. If the stock is consistently losing then it's probably not worth having in your portfolio.

STOCK OPTIONS

There are different ways to make money trading options. Options are one of the most versatile financial instruments, and they can be used by nearly any investor to complement his investing strategy and goals. Let's look at some of the ways you can trade options to make money.

1. Buying Calls

When you buy a call, you are betting that the market will rise in the short term. You can usually buy the option to buy a stock at a fraction of the price that you would need to invest in order to buy the full stock. This gives you the opportunity to experience massive profits if the stock rises, but you also run the risk of losing much of your money if the stock stays the same or drops in price.

2. Selling Calls

It is also possible to make money by selling calls. When you sell a call, you are paid a small premium in exchange for assuming the obligation to sell a stock if it reaches a certain price. If you own the underlying stock, this is known as covered call writing. If you don't own the underlying stock, this is known as naked call writing. Generally, a call writer (seller) hopes that the stock will remain the same or sink in price before the expiry date so that he can keep the premium.

3. Buying Puts

Frequently, puts are utilized as protection by somebody who holds the basic stock. A put enables them to offer their stock at an ensured cost on the off chance that it sinks. Be that as it may, you can likewise purchase puts regardless of the possibility that you don't possess the stock. In the event that you purchase a put on a stock which promises you the privilege to offer a stock at $80, and the stock sinks to $60, at that point you can purchase the stock available and exercise your choice, in this way acquiring a moment $20 per share benefit.

4. Selling Puts

It takes two people to complete a put contract, and the seller can definitely make some money as well. Selling puts is a bit like selling insurance. You collect a small premium, and if the stock drops below a certain price, you guarantee that you will buy it at a previously agreed upon price. Many stock investors will say that selling puts is one of the riskiest option strategies available because your profit potential is limited to the premium you collect, while you can lose a ton of money if the stock falls to zero. Other investors, such as Warren Buffett, exclusively sell puts. They sell puts on stocks they would like to buy but don't because the price is currently too high. Buffett only sells puts on good companies, so he knows there is little chance that it will fall to zero.

INVEST IN STOCKS - THE BETTER WAY

With so different type of financial instruments available in the market, there are a lot of opportunities to invest your money and earn huge profits. Certainly, the magnetism of stock market attracts everybody and of course, you can also invest in stocks to make money and fulfill your financial needs. Well, in the opinion of some big-time investors, the better way to invest your money is investing in stocks. The simple reason behind such opinion is the high rewards that you receive is your stock soars on the charts.

So, if you are also among the confused beginners who often ask themselves "where to begin," then you will find the answer to your question. There is a pool of information that keeps on flowing in from different sources like television, newspapers and of course internet. Such pool leaves you at the beginning and you don't know where to start. Before proceeding with anything, you must ensure that you do not want and cannot afford to make any mistake at this stage and for that, you must learn every aspect of investing.

The first step that you can take is to define your investment goals. The stock market, again, offers you a wide array of opportunities to make money. However, it is only possible if you define investment goals, make a suitable plan to begin and play the game with pure dedication and patience. So, ask yourself "what is my investment goal." You must be clear in your mind that you are investing in stocks to earn a regular income or want to get a capital gain on your investment. To be precise, your goal is a long-term investment or short-term investment. Different people have different requirements and, hence their investment goals are also different. Identifying your goals will help you get a proper vision and path to proceed. It will help you design your investment plan.

The next step is to decide how much money you can risk. It is very important for you to plan on your risking money. You must invest that much which you can afford to lose. It does not mean that you will not make money investing in stocks but it is a part of the safe investment plan. Stock market conditions are uncertain and therefore, as a smart investor your investment plan and strategy should be safe.

To determine the money you can risk, you can take a test called as "sleep test."

The next stage arrives where you have to plan whether you want to manage your funds yourself or interested in hiring an investment manager. If you are aware of rules of the game of stock investing and have acquired in-depth knowledge of different techniques, strategies, tools, etc. then you must manage your funds yourself and earn good profits. However, investment managers are also there to help you invest in stocks. They take care of your portfolio and take decisions to buy or sell your position.

If you choose to manage funds yourself (which is, of course, beneficial) then you must locate a good full-service brokerage firm or a discount online brokerage firm. The difference between the two is that the full-service brokerage firm charges you a solid fee in return for a full package of services including market research and order processing. On the other hand, discount online brokers provide information, news, live quotes and online trading platform for a commission on each order that he execute for you.

Online discount brokers are certainly better if you know the game.

Next stage for you is to create solid, risk-free investment portfolio. To do this, you must spread your risk by investing your money in different stocks. You must invest in stocks on the basis of your interest (sectors/industries of your interest and expertise) and of course, after analyzing the individual stocks after undertaking the technical and fundamental analysis. Once you selected the stocks and made your portfolio then you must keep the track of performance of your positions regularly. In case your stock is not performing up to your expected level than before you lose all your money, just sell it.

The last step is experience and patience. With experience, you will become a better investor while patience is the key to making money in stock market. Always invest and trade free from emotions. A controlled stock investor is a better player and makes huge money.

STRATEGY FOR INVESTING IN STOCKS

Investing in stocks is not like playing a game of blind man's bluff; neither is it a matter of trial and error. If you leave your earnings to chance or luck, you are more likely to lose than gain.

If you want to make money from stocks, you must draw a carefully considered plan. You have to create a stable, long-time, profitable investment strategy. Your broker may have provided you with certain investment tools and facilities, which may include low commissions, automatic investment plans, low-cost real-time trades, various research tools and easy account management. You can make use of these tools and plans to devise your strategy.

You have to develop your strategy on the basis of your objectives. First of all, you should decide your objectives for investing in stocks. Do you want to invest in stocks to create an additional source of income? Do you want to make it a full-fledged source of income? How much do you want to earn per month? Are you a long-term or a short-term investor? Above all, what is your budget and how often can you comfortably invest? If you were a salaried person earning, say, $3,000 per month, it would not be a good idea to invest $500 per week. Just decide upon an amount that you can afford easily without having to stretch your resources too far.

Diversify your stock investment

'Never put your eggs in one basket' is a time-tested adage. The stock market offers numerous options. Therefore you should follow the concept of diversification in the stock market also. Diversification in this context means spending your investment across different sectors and funds. If one sector shows poor performance, your entire investment will not be affected adversely. The risk exposure to a particular investment would be reduced and overall risk to your portfolio will be considerably minimized. To explain it, let us say you have invested $1,000 in one stock and the prices of your stock fall, you will be losing a substantial part of your investment. If, however, your investment is distributed over a number of stocks, you may gain in some other stocks. Thus your losses will be neutralized to some extent.

Invest in ETFs

The best and the most popular options are the low-cost index-tracking exchange-traded funds-ETFs. The ETFs are, in fact, securities that track an index or follow the performance of a group of stocks. They trade like regular stocks. The only and the important difference is that you have to pay minimal expenses for trading. It is, therefore, convenient and cheap to buy and sell the ETFs. Since they follow indexes like the **NASDAQ** 100 or the Standard and Poor 500 to track a bunch of different stocks, they are automatically diversified. The great benefit of buying ETFs is that you can actually buy hundreds of different stocks with every dollar you invest. You have to pay your broker only a low-cost investment plan fee that ranges from $1 a trade to $3 a trade.

Fractional Shares

If you think you cannot buy high priced stocks because you are intimidated by their high prices, you may consult your broker. You may be offered a plan in which you can buy fractional shares. In fractional share investing, you need not buy 100 shares or even one share. You can buy just a fraction of a share. Therefore you can invest absolutely any dollar amount with no minimums and buy any quantity of a stock or ETF. You can buy a thousand shares or one-tenth of a share through automatic investment plans.

You can buy expensive stocks with small investments. Let us suppose, a stock is trading at $200 and you can afford to invest only $50 per week. If you use the automatic investment plan offered by your broker, you can buy any fraction of a share at a cost as low as $1 per trade. In this way, you can invest in stocks of over 500 companies with only a few dollars by buying fractional shares of an ETF or any stock for that matter. This is really a revolutionary concept in stock trading.

Tactics and Tricks on How to Invest in Stocks

Evidently, one of the most profitable and easiest ways of growing wealth over a long period of time is by owning stocks. In fact, every Forbes 400 list holder has been bagged by a large portion of shares in either a public or a private firm. However, not everyone is the master of this trade and knows the tactics and tricks of investing in stocks. If you are one of those, read below to discover how to invest in stocks:

Invest only when you have:

The most important asset you require for investing in stocks is "money." Thus, a person should not invest in stocks until he has a secure job and a decent amount of their bank balance to sustain his daily expenses for a period of about 6 months.

Get to know what "Stock" is:

Before getting your hands on investing in stocks, it is very important that you have a basic idea about the terms associated with stocks. Thus, read different books related to stock investment before actually plunging into the real market.

Think before you invest:

One of the most successful executives in the world remarked once, "Always think again after thinking once." Only if you can pen down enough reasons for buying a stock, you should buy it, or else you should not.

Practice makes a man perfect:

When asked about how to invest in stocks, one of the most viable answers that emerge is "through practice." Always practice trading stocks on paper, before using real money. Begin with recording the stock trades, the trade dates, the share number, prices, profit rate, loss rate, etc. Only when you are comfortable with trading on paper should you start trading with real money.

Find a good broker and open a stock brokerage account:

This rule runs completely on a trial and error basis. Figure out a good broker based on his commission charges, total involved fees, the online reviews, etc.

Create a small portfolio of about 30 stocks:

Carefully analyze the stocks of various companies and select the top companies, which have come up with at least a little earning in the past ten years and have paid some dividends in the past 20 years approximately. Once you have sorted out the list, you can head towards making the investment.

Stay updated:

Most importantly, stay updated on the various investing websites like Fallen Angel Stocks or Motley Fool for getting information about the latest deals in the stock market.

WHY INVEST IN STOCKS

On this time of economic uncertainty, it is ideal if you understand how to make investments in stock. There are approaches to obtain a stock market education which might enormously increase your probabilities of utilizing stock tips to your economic advantage. If you will need your automobile repaired, you never ask the man with the neighborhood theater for assistance, you go to a licensed mechanic. Likewise, when you are serious about investing stock, you will want to receive stock tips from someone who offers a superior stock market education that you just could trust your hard-earned dollars to.

If you're determined about investing stock, there are several helpful ideas that will assist you to gain a stock market education even though rewarding yourself with the stock tips which can be beneficial.

1st, visualize it as shopping for the business alone instead of simply investing stock in the firm.

2nd, your objective is to become profitable whenever following stock tips, make sure the company is rewarding and that means you are usually also.

Third, a bit of stock market education could well be that you simply really should not invest the total % of one's assets towards stocks. Broaden.

Fourth, implement your own wise practice. An excellent stock market education could be really worth in excess of a sizzling stock tip in case you listen to your own interior wisdom.

Finally, in case your tendency is investing stock to grip to for just an amount of years, make sure to look at in on your stocks and think about getting rid of those if they are not providing like you may need.

Investing stock is usually a quite satisfying pastime if you understand when to join and when to leave. For those who have a passion for one thing like basketball as an example, take into account obtaining by yourself a stock market education inside the enterprise who produces the basketballs or even the basketball shoes. By doing this, you are going to preserve informed on the most up-to-date and biggest within your preferred activity, in addition, learn when to work with the stock tips to get or trade the commodity.

There are many people who stays inside the U.S. are used to residing paycheck to paycheck. Not that we want to or specifically delight in coping paycheck to paycheck, yet we do not hold the stock market education to alter it. If you figure out how to make investments in stock you can be in a position to conserve capital in your case and your family's long-term.

BEST TIME TO INVEST IN STOCKS

The issue is not really the best time to invest in stocks; but rather the best time to invest in stocks more aggressively. To succeed in stock investing, there are two basic signals you should watch. They can tell you when to invest more heavily in stocks and stock funds... because they are selling cheap.

Average investors should invest in stocks or stock funds on an ongoing basis, allocating a percentage of their total investment assets to this class of investments depending on their risk tolerance. Sometimes when the stock market makes you the most uncomfortable, it's the best time to invest in stocks and increase your position there. Many investors do the opposite. They sell near the bottom, take a sizable loss, and lay low until the market is well on its way to recovering past losses. That's a stock investing recipe for losing money.

If you were an investor in 2002 or in early 2009, you know what discomfort and the feeling of financial panic are. It's not easy to force yourself to buy when everyone else is running for the nearest exit. Here are two things to watch for, to give you more confidence in making the decision to buy more stocks when they are cheap.

First, you've got to follow a stock market major index when a falling market is making the headlines. Either the Dow Jones Industrial Average (the DOW) or the S&P 500 Index will do. If these have been down for one to two years it's time to pay close attention. If they are down 30% or more from the previous high it's time to get ready to buy. When selling escalates and prices then appear to be in a free-fall, it's time to **START** buying in increments.

Second, pay attention to the **P-E RATIO** for the major indexes. This ratio of stock Prices to corporate Earnings, P/E, tells you whether stock prices are cheap or expensive relative to the profits or earnings that justify their value. For example, historically a **P-E** of about 15 has been normal for our major indexes. This means that the price of stocks in the index is 15 times the earnings per share recently reported by the corporations in the index.

A ratio of 15 means that stocks are selling for 15 times earnings, as prices fall and/or earnings increase our ratio gets smaller and stocks are cheaper... and when prices rise or earnings fall stock prices get expensive. When the market's P-E gets higher than 20 times earnings it's pricey. At a P-E of 10 or less, stocks are basically cheap.

The best time to invest in stocks and start some serious buying is when both of the above conditions spell STOCKS ARE CHEAP. When the major stock market indexes have taken a beating and the P-E ratio gets below 10 it's time to buy - not sell stocks and/or stock funds. Keep a level head and buy in increments with a plan.

WHY INVESTMENT IS A MUST FOR EVERY INDIVIDUAL

You have been working in a company for the last five years. But why is your account balance is low? Do you invest? If you are not aware of the importance of an investment plan, you must wake up now. Think what will happen if you need money urgently - in such a situation, your savings will only help you come out of that grim situation. Those who do not understand the need of financial security often face problems. So, why welcome such problems - invest now and live happily all through your life.

In today's competitive world, there are several investment options available. But, which one is most beneficial is a million dollar question. No doubt, online trading today is a better option as compared to other investment options. Being online, anyone can invest and trade from any corner of the world. And if you have your own laptop and an Internet connection, then you can start trading at any place such as at your home or on the beach.

In addition to the easy trading system, online stock trading is also safe. All transactions done by the trader are kept secured on the Internet. Since you operate online on the stock trading company website, security tools installed on the website provide more safety. And once you log in to your account, you get attached with an online stockbroker who actually does all kinds of transaction, once you tell him to do. Brokers also provide valuable information such as information about major company shares, market moods, when to buy and sell stocks and more.

So, if you have really planned to invest in stocks then the first step you would need to take is to make a proper investment plan. This may include the amount you want to invest, for how long you want to invest and finally, how much profit you expect from your investment plan. You can definitely measure these things, at least up to some approximation. And it is always better for new investors to discuss their plan with online financial experts.

If your groundwork is perfect then you can proceed further easily and without any hassle. The next step you would need to take is to learn more about the market. There are various open resources available on the Internet - read the content and know the volatile market in a better way. It is really important for every investor to understand the volatile nature of the market. And the best way to understand is through market analysis. Today, company websites come equipped with trading tools - analyze the data and then trade accordingly. The stock market analysis will give you a view of the share price fluctuation rate to some extent.

There are many investors who do not follow these strategies and often fail to enjoy the benefits from their investment plan. So, don't follow them - it is not only the trading system where you need a good market knowledge - even if you want to sell a particular product in the market, you need a comprehensive market report, which may include the demand for that particular product, competitors for that product and so on. So, learning is important. Gain knowledge about the market, invest intelligently and enjoy the benefits, always.

CHAPTER FOUR
HOW TO MAKE MONEY IN STOCKS COMPLETE INVESTING SYSTEM

A "stock" - more commonly known as a share in some parts of the world - means a portion of ownership or equity in a company. As such, a stockholder is essentially an owner of that company with specific rights and obligations. Companies list on the stock market - or more precisely, a specific stock exchange - to sell their equity to the public, and thereby raise the capital they can use to grow their business. Once a company has listed on a particular stock exchange its shares can be traded on an ongoing basis by investors and traders alike.

While people often talk about "the stock market" they are usually referring to either a particular (physical) stock exchange where companies' shares are available to trade... or the sum total of the world's stock exchanges. In other words, if someone claims to trade the stock market, they may be referring to the general principle of trading stocks, or they may be referring to trading shares on a specific stock exchange. Stock exchanges can be large or small, depending on how many companies are listed, and the value of their share capital. The major stock exchanges are the Tokyo Stock Exchange, Frankfurt Stock Exchange, New-York Stock Exchange, London-Stock Exchange, Shanghai Stock Exchange and the Bombay Stock Exchange

Buying and selling shares involve contacting a stockbroker and asking them to settle the trade on your behalf. In return for facilitating this transaction, they will take a commission - either a flat fee or a percentage of the value of the order. You can call a broker via telephone or simply place your order on their website (most brokers have websites to enable this).

So how do you actually make money in stocks? Well, there are a number of ways, but a lot depends on your goals. If your objective is to invest for the long-term then you might take the view that, over time, a company's share price reflects its financial value. If you buy now, and the company's performance improves, your stock holding should be worth more in the future. You can either cash in the profit you've made or keep the stock in the hope that it will continue to rise in value.

In fact, this is the perspective generally taken by "fundamental investors" to make money in stocks. Fundamental investors use fundamental information about a company (primarily its financial performance) to justify buying, holding or selling stocks. Fundamental investors tend to hold their investments for several months at least, often a few years, and in some cases decades.

The other main type of investor is not really an investor at all - he or she is really a "trader". A trader typically rejects a long-term approach and seeks to make money in stocks by taking a much shorter term view. Since, in the short-term, prices of stocks are much less indicative of a company's value, there is often little point considering all the fundamentals. What matters is the market's perception of value, not necessarily a company's real value.

Given the capriciousness of the stock market in the short term, traders often prefer to use "technical analysis" - the art and science of evaluating price data - in order to issue trades. Technical analysts study price trends - depicted in charts - and draw conclusions about where the price might go next. Then they buy, sell or hold on that basis.

Both "fundamentalists" and "technicians" can make money in stocks. One of the world's wealthiest individuals, Warren Buffet, is a well-known advocate of investing on the fundamentals. On the other hand, there are many traders who swear by a technical approach. In particular, technical analysis holds an allure for many people who are excited by the idea of using a "super secret" trading system to make huge profits.

Trading systems can vary widely. Essentially, a trading system is the step-by-step approach used by a trader to make money in stocks. While there are general approaches to trading e.g. trend following, candlestick charting, and others, any given trading system is likely to be tailored by the trader to suit them.

There's no question that it's possible to make money in stocks. It's also possible to lose - so it's a good idea to learn as much as you can about stock market investing and trading.

HOW TO MAKE MONEY ON STOCKS WHETHER THEY GO UP OR DOWN

The super-rich grace their offspring with a financial education most of us cannot even conceive of! For those of us who were not taught the strategies and secrets of the super-rich, this article is for you!

Ever wonder why it is so easy for some just to make money out of thin air? They have been given a financial education, an education for life and this includes an education in finance and investing.

This is not the sort of information most of us pay a financial adviser for. The same financial adviser that is paid commission on the shares he sells for the companies he represents! The same companies that give us a small yield after years of investing whatever hard earned money we have left to invest after we have paid income tax and the interest on our mortgages. Kids of the super-rich don't use financial advisers: they are given a real financial education that isn't based on letting our money sit in stocks hoping and praying they will go up over time. The super-rich makes money regardless of whether or not their shares go up or down: providing you follow a few basic - yet little-known rules.

The super-rich is taught about the options market, about options strategies and options trading. They are taught about CFD's (contracts for difference) and they use strategies like 'channeling' and 'leverage' to make monster returns. Sound confusing? Hang in there, it's not; and it gets easier and can change your life and that of your loved ones.

Here's the good news!

- You don't need a huge outlay to make a lot of money and even replace your income!
- You can generate a constant cash-flow! You don't have to stress about whether or not your shares are going up or down you can make money no matter what. There are people waiting to rent your yet to be purchased or current shares and pay you for it. So even if the share price stays the same you still make money.
- You can take out insurance on your shares so you can't really lose!
- Strategies like 'channeling' and 'leverage' can generate you an 80% P.A. return and double your profit!

Having several different trading strategies within a portfolio maximizes flexibility and versatility enough to generate consistent profits in a variety of market conditions. Learning different strategies involving a variety of products enhances your profit capability and reduces your profit risk.

PROS AND CONS OF STOCK TRADING

Whenever a company issues stocks, it is an attempt to raise capital in order to invest in some endeavor. All over the world, the stock market works on this basic premise. When a company needs money, it will simply offer the stock and the options thus purchased will entitle the stockholders to a percentage of the profits, once the entire concern gets going.

The Internet has made things much faster and removed all geographical restrictions. Trading now takes place 24/7 because some part of the world is always busy with business. The Internet also makes it easier for anyone to take part in stock trading. Leading stock market firms also send daily emails with tips to their customers on how the market is expected to move today.

Everyone has heard about stock trading but very few people actually know the advantages of getting involved. Like any business venture, stock trading is not all advantageous and it is important to know both the pros and cons of stock trading.

Pros

Instant Returns

Active stock trading means you get an almost immediate return on investment. You get better returns in a short time as opposed to buying and holding your investment for years at a stretch.

Choice

Through the Internet, you can trade in any part of the world. You have no restrictions on the type of stock you trade in or what currency you trade in. You can browse the Internet looking for constantly moving stocks.

Familiarity

You already know most of the companies offering stocks so you are not on the strange ground. With a little time, you can understand the micro-dynamics to trade effectively.

Cons

Leverage

Stock trading leverage is very low when compared to Forex trading or futures trading.

Short selling

There is a rule against short selling that entails waiting before the price picks up again. This essentially limits the amount of profit a trader can make. There is no such constraint in Forex trading.

Costs

There is a substantial cost associated with stock trading that is unique to this market. This can quite often make stock trading impossible for almost everyone. You will need some amount of money before you can start investing in the market.

All trading - stock, Forex, futures, involves some amount of risk with their own sets of pros and cons. It is up to you as a trader to evaluate all these issues before you begin trading.

THE PROS AND CONS OF PREFERRED STOCK

There are cons and pros of investing in preferred stocks. Investing in preferred stocks is one way to assuring a continuous stream of income in the shape of dividends. What this means is that you are assured of a dividend income that may not be available to a common stockholder. Now, as an investor, you must be familiar that there are two types of stocks, common stocks, and preferred stocks.

Preferred stocks are a hybrid between a bond and equity. You got the right to a dividend income and this dividend should be paid before any dividends are paid to a common stockholder. These types of stocks can be converted into common stocks. The company fixes the ratio at which the conversion can be done. For example, for one share of these types of stocks, you may be able to get two shares of the common stock or even more.

Another plus point of holding these types of stocks is that in case of a liquidation, you as the holder of these types of stocks will be given preference in the payment of assets as compared to the common shareholder. Now, preferred stocks can be of two types known as Cumulative and Non-Cumulative.

In case of cumulative, if the company fails to pay the dividend in the stipulated period due to various reasons, this must be paid at a later date by the company. So in essence, the dividends accumulate with each period that might be quarterly, semi-annually or even annually. When the dividends are not paid, dividends are said to have passed and accumulated as areas in case of the cumulative stocks. In case of noncumulative stocks, if the dividends get passed, you don't get any arrears. You lose the dividends forever.

Whenever, the company declares a dividend, preferred stockholders get the first right to get those dividends paid and after that common stockholders get their dividends. These dividends get paid as a percentage of the par value or a fixed percentage.

Now, there are a few cons of investing in these types of stocks. The most important are that you don't get any voting right with these stocks. These types of stocks are sometimes issued by the companies to prevent hostile takeovers. So, as common stock holders have the right to vote but as an investor in these types of stocks though you get preference in getting dividend payments you don't get the right to vote.

Another disadvantage of these types of stocks is that they can be called anytime by the company after a certain date. You can't do anything if the company decides to call back these stocks after that date. Preferred stocks get thinly traded as compared to the common stocks.

Whatever, there are always pros and cons of investing in any asset. In case, you are looking for a fixed income stream like that you get for a bond then these types of shares should be included in your investment portfolio. Now payment of these dividends is however at the discretion of the company board of directors. If the company is facing cash problems, the board of directors may decide not to declare any dividends.

This is unlike that in the case of bonds where the payment of interest is guaranteed and the bonds are issued with the protection of an indenture. So even if the company is facing cash problems, the interest payment to the bondholders has to be made, but not in the case of these stocks. Another difference between preferred stocks and bonds is that interest payments are made through before-tax profits whereas dividends are paid through the after-tax profits.

CHAPTER FIVE
HOW TO DEVELOP THE TIME AND MONEY MANAGEMENT

Learning how to manage money is the most important thing that a person can do for themselves. Consider it, in the event that you don't know how to deal with your cash, you will just as easily lose all the money that you worked so hard to make. What people do not realize is that money management is something that is **LEARNED**. It's like a muscle, the more you use it, the stronger you will be at it. Getting stronger at managing money is essential to survival in today's world. There are plenty of news stories about athletes and lottery winners that lose their entire fortune in a few years. Why is this? They do not know how to **MANAGE**

money. They are living proof that even the richest people can lose everything they have if they don't learn this very important skill.

Before looking up money management advice, it is important to figure out exactly WHAT it takes to effectively manage money. It's really simple actually. There are only two things a person truly needs to manage money properly. Those things are a plan and self-discipline. That's it.

Have a plan. We all have bills to pay. Plan your savings, plan your spending, be organized and track everything transaction that you make. Nobody else will take care of your money for you. Whether you use the computer or a notebook, track all your earnings and spending.

Have self-discipline. Of course it's okay to splurge on things every now and then, but first and foremost are the bills. If your money is running a little tight then do not buy that new LED TV. You really don't need a new TV, at the end of the day you need to pay the bills and the people charging you won't care if you don't have enough money to pay on time.

Now that we have the extremely basic stuff out of the way, let's get to some real money management advice! If you already follow these ideas, or something close to them, then you are already a good money manager!

The ability to manage money has to be learned, developed, and practiced on a daily basis. There are eight steps to successful money management:

- Have a savings account
- Have an emergency fund
- Get organized
- Decide what you want to do with your money
- Look at all available resources
- Decide how much money you are worth
- Find out how much money you make
- Find out how much money you spend
- Set up a plan for spending your money and stick to it
- Evaluate your spending plan.

Have a savings account

I put 10% of my earnings aside into the bank, and never touch it. This is your savings account. It's literally money to be saved and the best part about it, you gain money through interest the more money you have saved up. Don't touch this money; it's only 10% of your income. Let it grow.

Have an emergency fund

I save another 10% of my money but its purpose is different. This is the emergency funds. If your car breaks down or your toilet stops working, this is the money that you use to fix the problem. Why should you have both a savings account and emergency funds? It's because you don't want to spend all your savings on an emergency. Even with an emergency, you should still have saved up money. It's just a good idea to always have a backup.

Get organized

If you find trends, for example, you spend more money on fast food than you do on groceries, then you can plan accordingly. Find out the luxuries that you spend money on and then focus your money on things you actually need.

Mark your documents or the dividers for your scratch pad as per the sorts of records you keep. For instance, marks may be selected as takes after:

- Land records
- Dress care and data
- Duty records
- General family unit data
- Family papers
- Family unit stock
- Charge card and portion installments
- Protection
- Total assets proclamation
- Record of profit
- Business records
- Car
- Lodging
- Record of consumptions
- Area of lawful records

- Wellbeing records
- Utilities

Determine your objectives

Great money management starts with objective setting. Objectives give you bearing. They give you a reason for the way you spend your cash. Objectives persuade and support you as you progress in the direction of doing things that are critical to you. What are a portion of the things you need to finish amid your lifetime? Which of these cost cash? Set up an arrangement for how you need to accomplish these objectives.

How would you set objectives for spending your money? To begin with you have to consider the things that are imperative to you and your family. Read over the rundown beneath. Choose the things you and your family believe are most essential and place a "1" next to them. Place a "2" next to the things that are fairly vital. Place a "3" next to the things that are not vital to you and your family.

- Individual appearance (Clothes, shoes, cosmetics, hair)
- Culture (theater, films, move, and presentations)
- Employment achievement
- Renown
- Nourishment
- Protection
- Religion
- Instruction
- Family excursion
- Profiting
- Sparing cash
- Beginning another business
- Diversion
- Vessel, angling hardware
- Family unit furniture
- Transportation (auto, truck, cycle)
- New house/townhouse, condo)
- Wellbeing
- Family exercises
- Companions
- Paying off obligations

- Gems
- Drawing in inverse sex
- Diversion
- Other

As an individual, you may experience difficulty choosing which thing is more essential than another. It's much more troublesome when at least two individuals live respectively as a family and offer cash. They may not concede to what is vital. On account of this absence of understanding, it is at times hard to choose where cash will be spent.

When you choose what is vital to you, this list will enable you to perceive what you need to move in the direction of. For instance, on the off chance that you set a "1" close to another auto, your objective might be to purchase another auto. Objective setting includes more than choosing what's vital to you. To help recognize objectives, put forth the accompanying inquiries:

- What would I like to do with my money?
- What amount of will it cost?
- To what extent will it take to get that much money?

When defining your objectives, make a rundown. Record what you need to do with your cash. Make your objectives particular. Try not to state, "I need money financial security." Financial security isn't particular. Rather, ask yourself what it takes to be monetarily secure. Your answer may be to have $20,000 in investment funds when you resign in 20 years. Provided that this is true, at that point you have to put $44.30 a month in a 5 ¾% bank account every month for a long time. Your particular objective at that point is to spare $44.30 a month from now until the point that you resign. This is unmistakably characterized objective.

Your objective ought to be sensible, testing, and achievable. Is it feasible for you to remove $44.30 from your month to month spending plan and still meet your essential everyday costs? On the off chance that you can manage the cost of $44 a month, your objective is practical, testing, and achievable. On the off chance that you can just bear to spare about $20 a month then you may need to diminish your long haul objective from $20,000 to $10,000.

Objectives ought to be quantifiable and reachable inside a given day and age. Determine the date when you need to achieve your objective. You can't put a date on achieving budgetary security, yet you can spare $20,000 on the off chance that you place $44.30 in reserve funds for a long time. Your objectives ought to be yours. Try not to let another person set your objectives for you. You will be significantly more prone to achieve your objective on the off chance that it is something you truly need to do. Objectives are distinctive for every person and family. They change as you experience the distinctive phases of life.

When you set your objectives, picture your objectives in your psyche. See yourself living in that loft, for instance, or on the shoreline making the most of your fantasy excursion. Innovative wandering off in fantasy land puts your objectives into your subliminal personality. Once your fantasy is in your brain, you begin considering achieving that fantasy in ways you doesn't understand. You naturally observe approaches to influence your fantasy to wind up noticeably a reality. Fix in your mind the correct things you need.

As you choose your objectives, record your transient, transitional, and long haul objectives. (Utilize Worksheet A)

- Here and now objectives: the things you need to complete in the following week, one month from now, in a half year, or a year.

- Middle objectives: the things you need to complete in the following one to five years.

- Long haul objectives: the things you need to do in the following at least five years.

As you lost your objectives, choose which objectives you need to utilize your cash for first. As you set dates for achieving your objectives, ask yourself which objectives are the most vital and which are the minimum imperative. Put forth the accompanying inquiries as you choose which objectives you will move in the direction of.

- How essential is this to me and my relatives?

- How dire is this? On the off chance that today is September 16 and you owe $1,000 worth of assessments, paying your expenses is more pressing than paying off a $950 charge-card obligation.
- What will happen on the off chance that I don't deal with this objective? On the off chance that you owe a $700 charge card charge, paying it off $100 a month will cost you less cash in enthusiasm than paying $35 for 20 months. It might crush your financial plan to pay it off in seven months, yet it won't cost you as much cash.
- What will I have to achieve this objective as far as cash, time, vitality, aptitudes, information, and capacity?

Objectives are critical keys to fruitful cash administration. They can enable you to influence your fantasies to materialize inside a particular timeframe. Objectives control you so you utilize your cash to do the things that are essential to you.

Look at all available resources

To achieve your objectives, you'll have to take a gander at all the assets accessible to you. This will incorporate your own aptitudes and salary, and in addition other group assets. They may incorporate time, vitality, interests, information, group administration, or material products. Commonly, people group assets offer budgetary help and additionally free or minimal effort options for consumptions. Such things as the library, social occasions, wellbeing division, parks, and transportation offices give administrations and diversion to the entire family at practically zero cost.

Know how much you are worth

What amount of cash would you say you are worth? In the event that you included all that you possess and subtracted all that you owe, would you claim more than you owe? Or, then again would you owe more than you possess?

Your money related total assets are dictated by subtracting all you owe (your obligations) from the present market estimation of all you possess (your advantages). This data will be valuable while deciding your protection needs and while applying for credits, settling a separation, or arranging your money related future. On the off chance that you have to pitch a few resources for inspire money to pay obligations, your total assets explanation will give you a chance to perceive what resources you have and the amount they are worth.

Utilize Worksheet B to figure your total assets. Recorded underneath are a few rules to help you in ascertaining your total assets:

How much money are you worth? If you added up everything you own and subtracted everything you owe, would you own more than you owe? Or would you owe more than you own?

Your financial net worth is determined by subtracting all you owe (your debts) from the current market value of all you own (your assets). This information will be useful when determining your insurance needs and when applying for loans, settling a divorce, or planning your financial future. If you need to sell some assets to get cash to pay debts, your net worth statement will let you see what assets you have and how much they are worth.

Use Worksheet B to calculate your net worth. Listed below are some guidelines to assist you in calculating your net worth:

- Have a land operator evaluate the present market estimation of your home or influence note of the deal to estimation of houses in your neighborhood.
- Money got from relatives, companions, or the legislature as exchange installments, for example, Social Security

Utilize Worksheet C to enable you to list your sources of income.

Find Out Your Monthly Spendable Income

Discover how much cash you have accessible every month by finishing the accompanying advances.

- Locate your latest pay stub
- Take a gander at the measure of gross pay. Net pay is the measure of cash you acquire before conclusions
- Take a gander at the measure of cash heading off to every derivation. What amount of your gross pay goes to reasoning (what rate)?
- Take a gander at the measure of your salary. Your salary is your gross pay less your conclusions.
- Search for your aggregate spendable pay. Add up to spendable pay is your salary in addition to cash from different sources. (Utilize Worksheet D to figure your spendable wage.)

On the off chance that you have a sporadic salary, assess the aggregate you hope to make for the whole year and gap by 12. Keep your gauge low. Specialists, for example, sales representatives, agriculturists, craftsmen, and essayists have sporadic wages.

Make a spending arrangement for every month. At that point when you get a check, spend it as per your financial plan. In the event that you get a bigger than-anticipated check, stay with the first spending arrangement and put the additional in reserve funds.

Know how much you spend

What amount of cash do you spend for sustenance, lodging, transportation, garments, individual care, and different things? In the event that you don't know the amount you spend every month for these things, keep a record of your spending. Record all that you spend each day for a month, when you influence a buy, to record the amount. The sum doesn't need to be correct, yet sufficiently close to enable you to see where your cash is going. Utilize Worksheet E to enable you to see where you are spending your cash.

After you have a composed record of where the greater part of your cash is going, separate your spending into classifications: settled, adaptable, and different costs, spending can likewise be isolated into every day, week after week, month to month, occasional, or yearly costs. Recognize what sort of costs you have.

Know when and where you burn through cash so you can manufacture a sound cash administration program.

Settled costs: The cost things you pay a particular measure of cash for consistently for a specific timeframe, these commitments are typically upheld through a marked contract. A few illustrations are lease or home loan installments, disaster protection, long haul mind protection, home protection, and portion installments, for example, your auto note. For the greater part of these things, you can't change the measure of the regularly scheduled installment.

Adaptable costs: The cost things you have more control over. You choose the amount you will purchase and the amount you will spend. Adaptable costs incorporate nourishment, attire, gas, power, water, telephone, transportation, gas, auto upkeep, auto protection, individual care, therapeutic costs, decorations, family unit costs, training, and expert costs.

Incidental costs: The additional things you buy that may not be completely required. A few cases are music CDs, perusing materials, for example, magazines, and recreational exercises, for example, theater or motion picture tickets.

We're fortunate that every one of our costs don't need to be paid in the meantime. We spend some cash regularly. We spend some on a month to month, quarterly, semiannual, or yearly premise, utilizing Worksheet F, record when these costs are expected. At that point put aside enough cash so you can cover the costs when the bills come due.

A few cases of regular costs are property charges; auto, home, life and medical coverage; tag reestablishment expenses; and get-always. Month to month costs may incorporate house installment, auto note, and utility installments. Day by day costs incorporate transportation and tidbits.

Plan your spending

Do you have a composed arrangement to control your spending? If not, utilize Worksheet G to enable you to design your month to month spending.

To start with, record the measure of cash you need to spend every payday.

Utilize your data from Worksheet E to discover your month to month costs. Contrast them with the normal yearly uses of Americans as indicated by the latest Consumer Expenditure Survey Results in Table 1. This table in addition to your record of costs can enable you to choose the amount to spend every month. Utilize Worksheet H to recognize some approaches to alter your spending.

On Worksheet G, record the amount you might want to spend for everything. As you build up your arrangement, check whether you have permitted cash for the accompanying things:

Real costs and future objectives, for example, adding rooms to your home, purchasing an auto, getting props for your kids' teeth, paying for your tyke's instruction, and purchasing a watercraft, blessings, or furniture.

Crises, for example, supplanting a punctured tire, therapeutic costs, fender bender, joblessness, auto repairs, dental bills, house repairs, and apparatus repairs

Regular costs, for example, school supplies and garments; house, auto, wellbeing, life, and handicap protection; land charges; enlistment expenses for youngsters, for example, for sports exercises; family excursion; birthday and Christmas presents; and duties

Obligations or past-due bills, for example, financial adjusts, portion advances, and home loan Monthly costs, for example, reserve funds or ventures, lease or home loan, utilities, family supplies, sustenance, commitments, portion installments, and medicines

Day by day costs, for example, school snacks and supplies, tobacco, tidbits, and dinners out Miscellaneous costs, for example, municipal club duty; daily paper or magazine memberships; clothing; attire buys and repairs; theater tickets, film tickets, and other recreational exercises; and individual care.

Assess your spending plan

After you live with your spending design a while, look it over. In the event that you place $100 in reserve funds at the first of the month and took out $50 before the finish of the month, at that point perhaps you can bear to spare just $50 a month. That is **OK**. In any event you recognize what you can spare. Looking into your spending encourages you choose precisely the amount you can spend or spare. Survey your spending design consistently and reconsider it with the goal that it works for you. Put forth the accompanying inquiries when you choose to spend your cash:

- Is this the best utilization of my cash at the present time?
- Will this buy enable me to achieve my monetary objectives?
- Is there something unique I have to utilize this cash for?

Six Real ways to Make Money Online

In the event that you experience difficulty achieving your objectives, take a shot at restraining yourself to take after your spending design. A genuine responsibility and commitment to your spending design can enable you to deal with your cash better.

Six Real ways to Make Money Online

Table1. Average annual expenditures and percent of income by category

Income			
Annual	$9,974	$44,933	$149,963
Monthly	$831.17	$3,744.42	$12,497.92

Category	Income	Percent	Income	Percent	Income	Percent
Food	3,193	32	5,614	12	10,243	7
Food at home	2,138		3,210		5,186	
Cereals and bakery products	276		413		673	
Meats, poultry, fish, and eggs	532		749		1,172	

Dairy Products	227	358	540

Worksheet A
Family Goals

Goal	When	Total Cost	Amount Per Month	Completed
Short-term (within the year)				

Intermediate (1 to 5 years)	
Long-term (more than 5 years)	

Worksheet B
Net Worth Statements for Three Years

Assets Owned	20	20	20
Cash on hand			
Cash in checking accounts			
Cash in savings accounts			
Cash value of life insurance			
Savings bonds*			
Money other people owe you			
Furniture and appliances			
Miscellaneous personal property			
Cars*			
Home*			
Other real estate*			
Stocks*			
Bonds*			
Mutual funds*			
Government securities*			

Annuities and other retirement plans			
Other assets*			
Total Assets	$	$	$

Liabilities Owed

Mortgage and liens			
Car loan			
Installment debts			
Personal loans			
Life insurance loans			
Charge accounts			
Other unpaid bills	$	$	$
Total Debts			

Can your family:

	YES	NO
Decrease basic supply costs		
Cut down on dinners eaten out		

- Cut utilization of non-nutritious drinks
- Keep up current home
- Discover more prudent living quarters
- Go up against more home upkeep and repair employments yourself
- Dispose of employed help inside or out
- Utilize utilities and family unit supplies all the more precisely
- Abstain from purchasing new home furniture unless required
- Consider purchasing utilized furniture
- Select simple care family textures and apparatuses
- Spend less to clothe and individual care
- Cut down on excursions to magnificence shop or hair salon
- Buy a more temperate

auto

Cut down in the midst of a furlough travel

Utilize open transportation more

Cut down on costly diversions or exercises

Exploit free exercises

Make utilization of the general population library rather than memberships and acquired books

Utilize open recreational offices

Diminish commitments or make them proportionate to salary

Give fewer endowments or spend less on blessings

Cut back on confront estimation of extra security

Change over some extra security into annuity

Recognize what salary isn't burdened		
Keep show amass medical coverage		

List some of your own ideas for cutting expenses:

_____

_____

These are just the basics of money management advice. If you have a solid foundation of savings, emergency funds, and spending, then you'll always have money for everything that you use. Remember, your priority goes to your bills (credit card, car payment, rent, etc.), then living expenses (groceries, clothes, etc.), then saving (savings accounts and emergency funds). Just make this a habit and you will already notice that you always have a surplus of money.

TOP THREE MONEY MANAGEMENT: HOW TO RUIN YOUR FINANCIAL LIFE

Who needs money management tips on how to ruin their financial lives? Please raise your hand. No one? This is a sure surprise. Given the many people with money issues when we look at our families, relatives, friends, and associates, I cannot help but wonder that some of them actually did receive money management advice of this nature. Whatever it is, in case you are still keen to ruin your financial life, follow these top 3 money management tips for beginners and you can be sure to get the results!

First, forget about setting money management goals to address any financial concern. Why? Let me ask you a question. How many New Year resolutions have you made, and how many of them have you kept? Always be honest with yourself. See? That is exactly why trying to set a money management goal is a waste of time other than a way to kill off some brain cells.

I am not saying you cannot have dreams of retiring at the Bahamas and living the good life one day or something. Sure you can. No one is stopping you. Just do not waste time and energy going into the specifics like when you want to retire, how much money you need, and what investments will help you get there.

By the way, always dream big. Do not sweat the small stuff--small money included. Having the discipline to save for a TV or car purchase is unnecessary and could be bad for you. The satisfaction of achieving a smaller cash objective can be addictive. It motivates you to do more and more of it and that means work. There is absolutely no need to train yourself to build up funds little by little. All you need is a big win on the lotteries or horses you bet on to take care of everything.

Since we touch on the subject of savings, I might as well give you the second of the money management tips to wreak havoc on your personal finances: Savings is the last item you need to put on the shopping list. Spend all the money to your heart's desires regardless of your income resources. Whatever cash you have left--not that it is likely to happen if you heed this advice--at the end of the month can then go into the savings account. Putting aside a fixed amount or percentage of your money first only keeps the bank accounts growing and growing. What good can those savings do?

You do not need an emergency fund for sudden medical bills. You are in the pink of health. No worry of unexpected illness striking, isn't it? What about car accidents? Well, they only happen to the other unlucky folks. Besides, your driving skills are superb. You have zipped along the highway at 200 miles so many times without trouble. How about saving for retirement investment? Perhaps, except that you are still young and retirement is a long way ahead. It is not too late to start retirement planning 30-40 years down the road when you are in the 50's or 60's, right?

Instead of paying yourself first to build up the savings, think of all the fun and entertainment you are missing! So shop till you drop and enjoy life to the fullest with every penny you have.

Now is the perfect time to introduce the third and last of the top 3 money management tips to crash your personal finances: Never ever track your spending. You do not need to be reminded of your impulse purchases or bad spending habits which a good record system will reveal. Paper notebooks are for idle doodling and are not record books to track expenses. Computers are meant for games and online chats. Personal budgeting software like Quicken or Microsoft Money are best left to the accountants and have no place on your laptop.

So, what if you overspent and ran out of cash? No problem. The almighty plastics can take care of it. Simply whip out a credit card and charge your expenses to it. If need to, you can always apply for another one to extend your credit further. They are not called the credit cards for anything you know.

How about all the credit card debts you owe? No problem there either. After all, you can just pay the minimum monthly and push the remaining balances away for yet another month. The banks can slap all the interests and penalty fees they want on the outstanding balances. No hurry for full repayment so long as you do not have to pay it now.

There you have the top 3 money management tips: Do not set any financial goal, do not save first, and do not track your spending. Follow these money management strategies and you will more than likely succeed to enjoy the fruit of ruining your financial life. Ignore them or, worse, do the complete opposite of these money management tips to your peril. You will find yourself getting a handle on managing personal finances and fast on the track to financial wealth.

MONEY MANAGEMENT AS TECHNIQUES TO PROTECT YOUR MONEY

Basically, money management is a kind of strategy and technique that will boost your money. This technique will not only protect but also manage your money and finances. The creation of this system has been a create help to society, since that you can in trust your money in this system. This system will be your best partner that will never betray you.

Now let's talk about the uses of this said program. Money management can help you to protect your money, it can help you to manage your business and financials, it can make your money yield at its highest interest values, it can give you an assurance that you can have the best services that you can use in your business, it increases the income of your company that will be an advantage on your part and it helps you to not worry anymore about your expenses, business, and financial reports. These things are just the basic services that you can enjoy and have if you will use the said system.

There some difficulties in using this system thus, we will give you some short briefing in how to use the said program. In using it you should decide which software you will use so that you will surely be able to get the services that you need. The nest you should know or decide is how to manage your money will you let manage, so that the system will not know also their limitations. You should also the program know about your financial reports or your budgetary goals so that it will be easy for them to manage your money. Now if you are worried about giving your reports to the system, then don't be for the reasons that all of your information will be highly confidential.

If you are interested in availing the services of money management then you can always use the help and assistance of online websites. The online websites are considered to one of the easiest and fastest ways that you can use in anytime you want and anywhere you go. Thus, these websites have created the online money management program that will help you to easily protect your money and belongings by just clicking some buttons on your computer or laptop. The online money management is the quickest way that you can use in availing for the said program.

In availing for online money management you should consider some basic requirements such as you need to have your own computer that will act as your instrument in finding the best websites and your computer should have an internet connection since that it is an online program. These two basic requirements are what you need to accomplish.

7 KEY POINTS TO MONEY MANAGEMENT SUCCESS

When easy access to plentiful credit is gone and financial resources have been exhausted, people are suddenly faced with the realization that they are going to have to manage their money and potentially the way they live. Don't worry; money management does NOT have to be painful.

Here are SEVEN HIGH-LEVEL KEY POINTS to kick off a money management plan that I typically go over with my clients:

1. Get out and stay out of credit trouble. The credit card companies were created to put us in a compromised position so they can charge us more money, more fees, and higher interest rates. Put yourself in a strong position away from becoming victimized and abused by the credit card industry again - this means avoid using credit cards for discretionary items that could easily drown you with debt. Remember, the dirty secret is that they want your credit score to below.

2. Determine and list out the types of assets you have. If you're going to invest your money into anything, make sure they are income-producing assets. If you spend your money on cars and clothes and the like, you'll find yourself getting nowhere in life financially, that's an absolute.

3. Determine and list out the types of debts you have. How much do you owe in educational loans, credit card debts, home maintenance, etc.? Anything over 11 months is considered long-term debt on a Debt-to-Income worksheet and should be included. Paying bills on time doesn't mean you're on a budget and hoping everything will work out on its own is not a strategy! The reason that people don't do this on their own is that they don't want to confront this issue. However, this step is critical as it will enable you to know where you stand financially today and where to go next.

4. Determine your budgetary priorities using the bucket theory (identify and prioritize). The bucket theory is a budget system that enables you to prioritize your spending into 5 categorical buckets. Priorities from highest to lowest should be as follow:

- The first and highest priority bucket represents financial security and includes an emergency fund and savings plan based on the concept of pay yourself first. 10% of your income should be allocated to this bucket.
- The second bucket means food, shelter, clothing, and transportation. These are pay-as-you-go items and money spent on necessity items you'll need to sustain life.
- The third bucket contains family's insurance needs including life, health, and disability insurance, property protection, and things of that nature.
- The fourth bucket is the quality of life such as money spent on holidays, anniversaries, birthdays, celebrations, etc.
- The fifth bucket represents the investments, which inevitably, will become number one.
- Write out your budget. This means to actually draw your spending out and figure out exactly what it is and how much you spend on each of the categories above. Now let's go to income. Is your total take-home pay required to sustain that budget...enough? And was it

well over where you were able to allocate at least 10% to your emergency fund?

- Balance out your budget. Having gone through all the expenditures, most likely, your budget will not balance and we now have to scale things back starting with discretionary spending. This is where the pain really begins. It's easy to just poke fun and make jokes, but the reality is that when people are doing this, it's serious. Now we have to go about getting rid of things to make this budget balance.

- Manage Your budget. Managing your money day by day is a simple concept, however, is not an easy endeavor because it's a human issue. My perception of a budget is not pure numbers. There's so much psychology built into this, how people look at the numbers, how they manage their lives, etc. The goal is to control spending. This is where I teach my clients how to protect themselves from themselves so they can succeed with managing their budget.

The bottom-line is you can't arrive at making the right decisions without thoroughly investigating and knowing where you're coming from financially and this can only be done through proper money management. Money management isn't "kind of" important, it is everything! With the proper steps and guidance, putting together a budget and learning how to manage your money day to day doesn't have to be as painful as most people imagine it to be - the hardest part is getting yourself to do it.

The biggest accomplishment you'll gain from it all is being able to know where you stand financially so you can take back control of your finances and ultimately, be able to establish a solid financial foundation for you and your family so you won't be in a compromised position ever.

TIME MANAGEMENT

The most prominent quality of the successful people is, they are the best time managers, and use available time as the most important asset for them. According to Brain Tracy; 'Time management is Life management', so the case of managing your time is much more than a skill or ability. Those people who develop the habit of utilizing their available time in the areas, where the ROI is higher; indeed perform the best. Whether you talk about the personal life or professional life, your ability to divide the fair amount of time for every activity you involve in will ultimately determine the quality of your life.

It is generally said, we are living in the era of time constraints or time-deficit, where people do not find enough time to become as competitive as their peers are. I do not agree with this simply because of the fact that, there are thousands of people, who are still making millions, earning good repute, and developing relations and networks, so, if the deficit in general, why are those people so much successful, then the rest? If the problem is common and shared, why do some of them are performing extraordinary and getting the most out of the same 24 hours that we possess? Do they have 48 hours a day?

No, the case is not like this, indeed they too have the same 24 hours a day, 7 days a week and 365 days a year. However, they have developed the ability to use their time in an efficient way and hence; their return on that asset is higher than that of ordinary people. Some of the people are of the view that this type of skills and abilities are natural and cannot be cultivated or adopted. To some extent, this is true, that natural abilities and talent does play a very important role. However, this does not rule out the importance and significance of putting an effort to learn something.

All of us have the natural ability to learn, speak, live and read. Then why some people are more expert in speaking, reading or doing something that the rest? This is simply because of the fact that, they put extra efforts to learn more, and hence, they have more knowledge, skills, and abilities. Now, having said this entire let me put this in another way. Your ability to manage your time (indeed life) can be developed, sharpened and improved with the passage of time and a little but regular investment in your self-improvement.

Time wasters are only those people, who do not value there as well as other peoples' time. If you want to become successful time manager, (say life manager) you will have to understand the value of your time. Just remind yourself of the fact that a moment passed will never come again. Once you develop a sense of value for your time and life, you will start thinking differently and live successfully. This would indeed be the very start of a new life, the better one, the excellent one. Hence, developing a sense of value for time and life is an essential ingredient for the better life and time management.

Think that the time that passed will never come back to you again, so use it wisely. Invest your time more carefully than you invest your money because money can be regained but not the time. This only requires thinking a bit differently from the rest and if you can change your thoughts, you can definitely change your world as said by Shakespeare!

TIME MANAGEMENT - AN ESSENTIAL TOOL

In this contemporary era of hi-tech gadgets, autonomous bots and what not, it is essential to value our time. Especially after the economic downfall, when things didn't go the way they were planned. People have been working day and night to try to make ends meet. But one question still remains: Is all of our time being utilized efficiently and effectively to generate the intended result? The answer to this question is embedded in the aspect of Time management.

What is time management?

Managing your time is an imperative set of principles, skills, tools, and systems that work together to help you get more productivity out of a specific block of time as compared to the usual value. It is mostly concerned with prioritization and organization. Charles Darwin once said: 'A human who dares to waste one hour of life has not definite discovered the value of life.' We can think of the management of our time as a magical remedy to get our things done on time. Instead of working harder you should work smarter.

Importance of time management

Time management is undoubtedly one of the more necessary determinations to achieve success in life. It plays a radical role in you becoming a well-organized and progressive person. The concept of time management is not contemporary; as it dates back to ancient times. We have witnessed it in many aspects of our lives in various ways, but only a few of us actually succeed in understanding the real essence of time management. Although the real concept of time management is a bit hard to understand until you know the secret. Once you seriously decide to get down to it, it becomes very easy to incorporate in your life. This magical remedy can help you achieve almost everything in your life & the best thing of all is that it doesn't even require any additional resources or outrageous efforts.

Is Your Time Management Effective?

One of the reasons we need to manage our time is that most of us have specific goals or objectives in our life which we need to be accomplished in a certain amount of time. In order to fulfill that ambition, one might work around the clock or expend an extensive amount of effort, but still not get the expected result. It is because the method or technique in which this effort is being devoted is not properly engineered with respect to time management. Hence in order to achieve the adequate results, it is necessary to make sure the time management technique is effective.

In order to ensure effective management of time, one must be able to control his own will. We all know that there are many things in our life that distract our attention and waste valuable time. So, basically, managing time has a very close relation to self-management. A man with supreme self-control can acquire productive time management skills. To effectively manage time, prioritize your tasks in order of their importance. Make a plan for each task on your list. Execute the tasks accordingly and keep repeating the process for other tasks.

It is all about carving time out of the day and organizing the schedule efficiently to make the most out of it. Effective management of time also involves patience and practical thinking. Another byproduct of this method is that reduces stress and revitalizes your body; which enables you to work even more persuasively. It is virtually impossible to achieve all of our goals without following an effective time management technique.

WHAT DOES TIME MANAGEMENT HAVE TO DO WITH IT?

Do you ever wonder why so many people are overweight? Everywhere you turn you see advertisements about weight loss. How many of us have fallen for: "Join our club, eat our food and you will lose up to 30 pounds in 30 days", OR "Take this pill and lose the flab". With the upsetting realization that there is no quick fix. As soon as we stop our 30-day schedule of supplied food or our 30-day supply of the weight loss pill - we are right back where we started.

I believe the majority of our society knows that in order to lose weight we actually have to exercise and eat healthy foods. How hard can it be? So, let's do it. Let's exercise regularly and eat perfectly-zone meals, attain our BMI and become healthy Americans!

In reality, a small percentage can follow through with that goal. The majority of people will last less than a week. Once the weekend rolls around we are chomping down on pizza, drinking a beer and laughing with friends. Saying to ourselves " we'll start again on Monday". Needless to say, this is a never-ending process and sooner or later we are on our 16th Monday repeating the same inexhaustible story of our lives.

Why is it so hard to eating right and exercise regularly? The reasons....wait for it.... is poor time-management skills. Yes, I've said it. We have become a lazy society. We have time to check our friend's Facebook status 5 times a day, but when it comes to 25 minutes of exercise or preparing healthy meals- we don't have time. In essence, we are unable to prioritize our list of priorities and follow through with them.

It has been proven that there are higher rates of success for weight loss with people who organize their meals ahead of time; and write down in their daytimer when they are going to the gym. People who treat their personal time-management skills like their career will complete every task during their day - including losing weight. People who prioritize their time - and follow through with their schedule will undoubtedly succeed in most areas of their lives.

Oblivious to the reality that by organizing and following their schedule in such a way that they treat their food preparation time and gym time the same way they would treat their Grey's Anatomy time - the pounds would drip right off.

As society's number on the scale decreases, society's self-esteem increases and the cycle continue. We continue to follow our schedule and stay fit and before we know it we are a happier and healthy nation.

Here is a list of things to remember to do if you want to get into shape:

1) Get an organizer ASAP that lists the time of day from am to pm and start organizing your time. Highlight gym time in RED so you know nothing can take you away from that.

2) If it takes you less than 10 minutes to cook your food - you are not eating the right foods. Highlight in your organizer 1 hour a week to look for recipes online that contain ingredients that are located on the outside of the grocery store. The less you buy from the middle aisles of the grocery store the better. On a non-busy day spend some time and write in your day timer what meals you are going to prepare and make each day and **FOLLOW IT. PVR** your favorite TV-shows and watch them later.

3) Scratch out accomplishment after they are done with a smile.

3) Once a week treat yourself to a treat that doesn't add pounds - massage, new shirt, etc.

Follow this plan for life and you will not only have better time management skills, you will weigh less because you are moving more and eating healthier. Your self-esteem will skyrocket and no longer will you say: "I have no time" but rather with confidence "I have all the time in the world"

TIME MANAGEMENT SOFTWARE SOLUTIONS

With today's fast-paced living time management not only can save time but money as well. Now with the opportunity of being able to take advantage of Time Management Software, it can make life a whole lot easier.

What is Time Management Software? This is software that you can install on your computer quickly and easily. Although this software is applicable to both home and business when it comes to business it will no doubt be a great cost saver. Not only that, this software also helps you to get and stay focused on the important things you need to do most especially when it comes to your work.

There are different types of Time Management Software that you can find if you surf the Internet. There are several Time-Management-Software that offers you a free trial. This is a big advantage to you because you can try the software for free with no service charges for one month for example. Your job will surely be easier with a lot less stress once you have used the right tool and this is the Time Management

Software. This kind of software is easy to use; all you need to do is simply install it and learn the basics.

These are the advantages that you can surely benefit from once you install Time Management Software:

- It helps you to make use of your time wisely as well as effectively without wasting time. Not only that, it also helps you to organize your time so you will know which work you need to prioritize and focus on.
- It helps you to finish your work faster as well as more efficiently without any worries and problems; this is a big advantage to those who have lots of bulk work every-day.
- This kind of software also helps you to control your time so you can take on other tasks that you may not normally have been able to schedule in.
- Time Management Software allows you to organize your time so you have extra time to dedicate to your personal life such as spend time with your family.
- This software helps you to manage as well as handle your time, effort, and even your energy so you can

focus, concentrate as well as take time to the more important work that you need to do.

- This software also guarantees that you will be more focused productive, useful, as well as creative when it comes to your work since you are not feeling stressed when it comes to working. This is one of the most important benefits that you can get if you install Time Management Software.
- With Time-Management-software, you don't need to worry about important deadlines since this software will help you to manage not only your time but also keep you organized and structured.

TIME MANAGEMENT GOALS

Time management goals are something that more people need, and far fewer have an interest in discussing. So, in this article, we're going to delve deep into this topic.

What are time management goals? Well, there are two sets of time management goals: the first is the goals that you set while managing your time and the second is the goals that you set about how you manage your time.

So, let's begin with the first set: goals you set for yourself; the goals you're trying to meet. These time management goals are highly important for many reasons.

The first one being that the accomplishment of these goals is the point of managing your time. If you're not trying to accomplish these goals in a certain time, then why are you managing your time?

Second, the goals themselves determine the amount of time that needs to be spent on them. Well, the amount of time it's going to take you to accomplish them.

Third, the goals themselves are the things that will lead you to a determined passionate persistence or to procrastinate. Many people really want to do things; however, they fear the outcomes of it (fear of success) or the doing of it (fear of failure).

So, as far as those time management goals go, you need to pay attention them and their ramifications; however, it's also important to pay attention to the goals of your time management system itself.

What does this mean? Well, if you use a time management system, the system itself has a way of operating and a set of goals that determine how one is to act within that system. For instance, I use a task management system and it's set up to help you get your tasks done in order of priority. Which is why for instance, I'm sitting here first thing in the morning writing articles though I'd rather be writing sales copy--at this point in my life, traffic to my list is the most important thing I need to accomplish. Since I know that, I make sure to write articles first thing when I wake up.

As you do this and use the time management goals of the system you're using, it's also good to setup goals to inspire you to work in a more efficient way. For instance, I generally write articles from nine to one; however, I'm trying to cut it down to nine to eleven so that I can shove all of my week's traffic generation into the first three hours I'm awake and spend the rest of my day helping clients, making products, or hanging out with my great, but whimsical friends who like to invite me out at the drop of a hat. Regardless of what I do, I like that my time management goals help me to focus on what's most important and to get that done first so the rest of my day is fluid.

TIME MANAGEMENT EXAMPLES

Sometimes, my clients ask for time management examples because many people have trouble imagining what a time management system is supposed to look like actually functioning. And sadly, this information paralysis is a common side-effect of some personal development literature either because of an issue in the creation or the reading of the text (or audio or video or whatever). But rather than blame anyone, here are two examples of the major time management systems so you can see what they're supposed to look like.

The first system to discuss is traditional time management. This form of managing your time works by getting you to setup a schedule that's relatively similar everyday and has enough time to accomplish all of the tasks that you want to accomplish. The best way to start is to just schedule in the things that you must do everyday at a certain time, e.g. sleep, work, commute, etc. As these are already dead space you can't do anything with.

To use this form of time management, you'd first want to consider what you want to accomplish. Next, figure out how many hours you think that it's going to take you to accomplish it. (If you're sensible, you'll add an additional 10-30% just in case - if not, free time!) Then, schedule the hours anywhere that'll fit the things you must do like sleep or commute.

An example of this is the life of a normal nine-to-five person. They get up at seven, brush their teeth and shower by seven fifteen. Eat breakfast by seven forty-five. Drop the kids off by eight thirty. Arrive at work by nine. Work until noon; take a half an hour lunch. Work twelve thirty to five. Drive home by five-thirty. Eat dinner at six. The rest of the night is free until eleven (bedtime). Everyday is very similar and allows for higher levels of productivity.

The alternative form of time management is task management. This revolves your day around your tasks.

To use it, you just need to figure out what you'd like to get done and what you need to get done today. Write these down in their lists. Now, prioritize each list from most important to least important. Set a reasonable time to complete each task. Now, do the tasks in order of importance starting with the need to list.

An example of this is my day because I use a task management system daily. So, today looked like this: I need to work on my Hegel paper (one hour), write ten articles (three hours), finish Sean Mize lecture set (one hour), and cook dinner (one hour). And I'd like to clean my room and bathroom (one hour). I listed them in the order of priority I followed, so I don't need to readjust that. Now, I just need to go through and does each task in order with as much focus as possible so that I can get them done quickly and effectively.

THE IDEOLOGY OF TIME MANAGEMENT

Success in any aspect of life is reliant on time management, efficient time management. Time management is the key to successfully accomplishing tasks in accordance with a set schedule and reduces the likelihood of panic setting in. Many people believe that preparing a schedule to manage their time is a chose that itself eats up a lot of time. This may be correct to some extent in the short term but planning ahead will enable you to more easily achieve the outcome you have set in a more productive and time effective manner. When preparing a time management schedule there are some important points to consider:

Prioritize Your Workload

If you are working on various projects simultaneously it is advisable to set a priority for each project according to its importance. Then consider essential tasks and significant assignments closely related to each project. If you work with other people, assign tasks to each person and allocate a completion date for each and every task. At various stages of the project, revisit your schedule to confirm you are moving ahead according to the schedule.

Sort Out Low Priority Tasks First

From your priority list choose one of low importance to accomplish instantly which will reduce the number of tasks in the list. This will help to create confidence of achieving further tasks and enable you to proceed with the next task with your head up and confidence brimming. If you start with a difficult task, it can be more time consuming to achieve and can lead to a sense of non-achievement. Don't put off a task till tomorrow if you can do it today. Don't procrastinate! Procrastination will not help you achieve anything. This is very important and a highly relevant time management principle.

Miscellaneous Hints

Here are a few easy to instigate hints to help facilitate better time management. Make them part of your routine.

- Put your desk in order.
- Dispose of files which are no longer required.

- Keep files in use in a systematized manner with stickers or something similar to easily and quickly identify each file.
- Start using planners, organizers or diaries so that you are always on top of important occasions and meetings.

Determine the Worth of Time Management

Time is the most important and valuable asset in all over our lives so we all need to give it the importance it deserves in order to become successful in life through achieving our goals in the timeframes we stipulate. Time is as precious as gold - we would all love to have more and more of it. We know we can't generate more time, so the best we can do is to manage the time we have in an appropriate and logical manner instead of wishing for something that is simply not possible. It is an established fact and historically evident that people who constantly achieve success are highly skillful at adopting efficient time management principles.

Time management is basically the capability to put your time in order to enable you to meet your targets within specified time periods by keeping a priority list and taking it into consideration every time you do something. It is always easier to complete the less important and easy tasks first and leave the important ones till later because for the completion of comparatively easy jobs you don't have to put in the same amount of hard toil. And, despite less effort, you get the same sense of achievement and encouragement to complete rest of the jobs with confidence.

Time management not merely deals with the accomplishment of work in certain periods of time; rather it is the training to develop an ability to prioritize your objectives so they can be achieved in the shortest possible time. It is about discriminating amongst the priorities of what need to do and what is really required to be done. Many books and articles have been created focusing on the importance of time management and the ways of learning these skills. Keep a schedule of how to spend your day, week and so on and then carry out an honest self-assessment periodically: perhaps at the very end of each day week or each month to see whether you are progressing adequately against the goals you have set.

CHAPTER SIX
HOW TO CREATE A WEBSITE

A lot of people complain of how difficult it is to start a business. They often say that they can't go through with it because they can't afford to pay for advertisements. It's a good thing that the internet has opened up a lot of opportunities and taught people how to create a website for business. Aside from the fact that it's easily accessible, it's also convenient, because then, you won't have to invest a lot of money. All you have to do is look for a free web hosting site and pay the necessary fees if you need any upgrades.

If you are interested to learn more on how to make a website, here are some tips that will help you:

- If you want to learn how to create a website for your internet business, the first thing that you need to do is plan your content and design. Since your main goal is to draw more clients, your webpage should be attractive and interesting at the same time. Present your products well, so that customers will be encouraged to try it out.
- When you are writing article or content for your website, you have to be conscious of the things that you are posting. It would help if you make an initial draft and read it well before you upload it online. As the old saying goes, "don't make promises that you can't keep". This will prevent you from going through complicated problems in the future.
- The basic thing that you need to know when learning how to create a website is to make things simple. Don't add unnecessary things that will make your site harder to understand. As much as possible, stick with the basics, and make sure that your advertisements and webpage will attract your target audience.
- If you want to make a website to promote your business, you have to be consistent in updating it.

People would want to find out how credible you are based on the updates that you are making. You have to keep up if you want your clients to continuously visit your site and recommend you to their family and friends.

- If at some point, you decide to look for a hosting site that will allow you to expand, try to look for options and browse the internet first. Look for a good offer that will help you achieve your goals at the right price. If you have friends who are also in the same business, try to ask them for recommendations. They may be using something that you can put to good use.
- If you want your webpage to increase in ratings, the best things to-do are to build inbound links to other websites, doing this will give your site a bigger chance at being recognized.

Creating a website is not that hard, especially if you know exactly what you want. Set your priorities straight and establish clear goals, so that you won't be wasting time and money on things that are not important. If you want your business to be successful, you have to work hard for it!

BENEFITS OF CREATING A WEBSITE

More small businesses than ever are looking to establish a website presence in order to market their business, its products, and services. But you just can't think of how having a Web presence would benefit you, especially when the majority of your customers are local. If you are not sure that an Internet Presence would help you, then consider the following:

You have a service or product you would like to sell.

- Potential customers can obtain information about your product within minutes
- Provide a map and directions, showing people how to get to your physical store.
- Allow your customers to order from the convenience of their home.

You want to let people know about your business or organization.

- Reach more people than by handing out your business card.

- Serves as an online brochure - one can update immediately.
- Add your website visitors to your mailing list or newsletter.

You have customers who have questions or need your support.

- Your website is available 24 hours a day 7 days a week.
- You can provide great answers to Frequently Asked Questions.
- Provide phone, fax number, and address so your customers can contact you.

You want feedback from your customers.

- Use a feedback form to make it easy for your customers to give you their input.
- Conduct online product surveys.
- Conduct customer service surveys to find out how you can improve.

You want to expand your business, domestically or internationally or both.

- Utilize personalized e-mail and save $$$ on your phone/fax bill.
- You do not have to worry about being in a different time zone.
- You can offer your information in multiple languages.

You need to transfer information to other locations, salespeople on the road, etc.

- Create a password protected page so important information can be downloaded.
- Transfer document via website is cheaper and faster than by UPS, FedEx, etc.
- Unlike a fax, your documents arrive in color!

If you find that none of the above applies to you, then you should absolutely not waste your time and money creating a website. However, if you see how your sales, visibility and overall customer experience will benefit by having a Web presence, make creating a website a priority.

WEBSITE HOSTING

The expression website hosting is employed for the business of giving space or server and preserving files for one website or more websites on the Internet. Website hosting is also known as web hosting. Web hosting is a sort of Internet hosting service that lets people and businesses to gather their data, imagery, videos and all additional contents and make them available through the Internet.

You can locate all sorts of firms online which will provide hosting for your new site. They are referred to as web hosts, and they offer a variety of packaged services using the most modern technology for putting your information up on the Web. They include both your own space and the necessary internet connectivity. Such hosting falls into different categories: no-cost, graphics dedicated or shared.

With this type of hosting, files may be uploaded using FTP or internet interfaces. Clients may look for hosting providers after they gain availability to the internet with dial-up or broadband. This is provided to clients as a variety of formats based on their needs.

Website hosting services for special reasons recommend a commercial package, which features trade tools, sales correspondence, and the processing of credit cards. Dedicated hosting, along with managed website hosting, is quite popular for the clients' classy needs.

When it comes to website hosting companies, there are many options in the area. As such, finding the best website hosting company can be a challenge. But it is not wise to shut your eyes and pick just anyone.

Excellent web hosting services should be available to each and every person worldwide. To a large degree, the look and feel of your website will be determined by the hosting company you choose. Fortunately, there is numerous website hosting firms with excellent features and service records.

Packages for almost any budget are available from the numerous website hosting companies. From entry-level services to higher grade small business hosting packages for businesses and power users, every package offers the highest bandwidth, disk space, and server CPU power available today.

Website hosting is the practice of storing and delivering the various files and other components of a website to the Internet. There are a variety of options available to both businesses and the average person, including free and paid, and in addition to services for website files, there are also services available to store and deliver images. If you are running a business, a commercial web hosting company is recommended; as they offer tools that standard services may not. The companies that specialize in small business hosting make tools available for credit card processing and other similar features, in addition to offering dedicated and managed to host.

Six Real ways to Make Money Online

BEST WAYS TO MAKE MONEY WITH YOUR WEBSITE

When people start their first website they always think about their vision of the site and what they want to put on it, but they forget about the most important part of having a website, it has to make money. The reason a website has to make money is that most people have a vision where they get 1000's of visitors to their site daily and when this happens your cost of running the site will be a lot higher than it is with just 10 visitors per day. Now that you know why it is important to make money with your website, let me show you the 4 best ways to do it.

Google AdSense

The most common way to make money with your website is by using Google AdSense. The way AdSense works are Google pays you every time a person clicks on the ad on your page. Some ads will make more money than others, but this is by far the most common method to make money with your website. The trick to making a good amount each day is first getting a huge amount of traffic and also making the ads look like they are actually part of your site. I have found that it is best to place a big ad right in the center of the screen so when a reader sees's the page they will notice the add

Affiliate Promotion

This is by far my favorite and the reason is that you can make a huge amount of money from a single sale. For instance, if you have a site about making money online there are tons of products you can promote using ClickBank and some of them pay thousands of dollars for a single sale. It is great. If you have not tried affiliate promotions then you really need to, this one method will boost your income single-handedly.

Link Sales

Link sales are what most people never think of and I really don't know why. Selling links on your website is guaranteed money that will be there. If your site gets a lot of traffic then you can make a huge amount of money from just a few link sales. When it comes to link sales you need to give more than your competition that way you will be able to charge more and be able to hold at that price. This is a win-win for both you and the person buying the link.

Membership site

This is another method that many people never think of and the reason they never think of it or at least don't do it is that they think nobody will pay for what they have. Let me tell you something, you would be surprised what individual is willing to pay for. My very first membership site was about Baseball and how I made my site differently was I gave away 2 tickets to see the World Series. Word quickly got around that there was a site out there that charged $5 per month and would give away World Series tickets to a lucky member. I quickly reached over 1000 members and so once that happened I knew I had something great. Just think about what you can do with your site and give something away, people love that.

CONCLUSION

To be successful in online entrepreneurship, as is true with any business, you must be aware that "get rich" or "get rich quick" goals/hype is scams. You must be able to set achievable and measurable goals. And, most importantly, you must be able to do this on your own. You must have the resolve and determination to set, manage and achieve your own goals.

www.ingramcontent.com/pod-product-compliance
Lightning Source LLC
Chambersburg PA
CBHW020905180526
45163CB00007B/2635